southern SWEETS COOKBOOK

Down-home desserts from Our State magazine

Our State
NORTH CAROLINA

Designed by
Katherine Dayton

Photography and styling by
Matt Hulsman

Styling Assistants
Mandy Stovall
Katherine Dayton

Edited by
Elizabeth Hudson

Photographed desserts prepared by
Amy Lowe, Paulette Smith, and Wayne Atkins of the Guilford Technical Community College Culinary Technology program, supervised by instructor Michele Prairie

---

Published by Our State Magazine
Greensboro, North Carolina

Southern Sweets Cookbook

ISBN 978-0-9779681-7-6

Published by *Our State* Magazine
P.O. Box 4552
Greensboro, N.C. 27404
(800) 948-1409
www.ourstate.com

Printed in the United States by R.R. Donnelley
Cover photography by Matt Hulsman

Library of Congress Control Number: 2010928137

Guilford Technical Community College
Culinary Technology

Photography courtesy of VanderVeen Photographers

Instructor Michele Prairie (foreground) demonstrates a technique to Amy Lowe.

Under the direction of lead pastry instructor Michele Prairie, students in the Culinary Technology program at Guilford Technical Community College prepared the eight featured desserts in this cookbook.

The first school in the state to be accredited by the prestigious American Culinary Federation, GTCC's Culinary Technology curriculum prepares students for a variety of culinary careers, from sous-chef and executive chef positions to food service management, in a range of settings, from restaurants and hotels to resorts, clubs, and health-care facilities.

Students receive extensive hands-on experience in GTCC's top-of-the-line commercial kitchen and make everything used in food preparation from scratch, even ingredients like mayonnaise, puff pastry, and pasta, according to Joyce Hill, Department Chair of Hospitality Education.

For information on the curriculum, visit gtcc.edu. or call (336) 334-4822.

White Chocolate Cheesecake Tart with Cranberries | page 46

Contents

Bob Garner's Banana Pudding | page 8

Banana Pudding

Bob Garner's
Banana Pudding

'Nanas from Heaven

Rock Barn Women's Club
Banana Pudding

Dawn Scott's
Banana Pudding

Easy Banana Pudding

Bob Garner's Banana Pudding | Serves 8

Our State, May 2008

7 medium to large bananas, firm and ripe

8 eggs

½ tsp. cream of tartar

1¼ cups sugar

2 Tbsp. flour

¼ tsp. salt

4 cups whole milk

1½ tsp. vanilla

Pinch of freshly ground nutmeg

1 box Nabisco Nilla Wafers

1 pint whipping cream, plus additional ½ cup sugar if making the cold version

About this recipe: This recipe can be prepared with a meringue and served warm or prepared with whipped cream and served cold. To ripen bananas more quickly, put them in a paper bag and keep an eye on them until their skin speckles.

Custard

Separate eggs, and put egg whites in refrigerator to chill. Beat egg yolks by hand until smooth, then gradually whisk in flour, sugar, and salt. Gradually add milk, stirring constantly. Slowly bring to a near boil over moderate heat, continuing to stir, and cook until thickened (about 10 minutes). When thickened, remove custard from heat, and stir in vanilla and nutmeg.

Meringue

Beat egg whites and cream of tartar with electric mixer until frothy, then slowly add ½ cup sugar, continuing to beat whites until stiff.

Line bottom and sides of a 9-x-12-inch baking dish with Nilla Wafers. Cover wafers with a layer of sliced bananas (using about 3½ bananas). Spread half of custard over bananas. (If you're using whipped cream, next spread half of the whipped cream over the custard.) Make another layer of remaining Nilla Wafers, remaining 3½ bananas, and remaining custard. If using whipped cream, spread the remaining whipped cream over the top, and refrigerate for several hours. If using meringue, spread the meringue over the top of the custard, making sure to push it all the way to the edges and seal it so it doesn't shrink. Bake the meringue version at 425° for 5 minutes or until the meringue is browned, then let sit at room temperature for several hours before serving to allow the ingredients to blend and soften.

Longtime Our State *contributor Bob Garner has explored hundreds of North Carolina restaurants; here, he shares a favorite recipe from his own kitchen.*

'Nanas from Heaven | Serves 8-10

Our State, August 2006

2 3.4-ounce boxes vanilla pudding (not instant)

1 12-ounce box of vanilla wafers

4 to 6 very ripe bananas, sliced

For meringue:

4 egg whites

½ tsp. cream of tartar

6 Tbsp. sugar

1 tsp. vanilla extract

Preheat oven to 350°.

Prepare pudding according to package directions. In an oblong glass baking dish, put a layer of vanilla wafers on the bottom, then bananas, then pudding; repeat with wafers, bananas, pudding.

For meringue: In a separate bowl, beat the egg whites until frothy, then add cream of tartar, and beat until peaks begin to form. Beat in the sugar, 1 Tbsp. at a time until stiff, then add vanilla extract. Spread over the pudding, and bake just until brown, about 15 minutes.

Allow to sit for 5 minutes before serving.

— Hungry for Home: Stories of Food from Across the Carolina *by Amy Rogers. John F. Blair, Publisher, Winston-Salem. 2003.*

Rock Barn Women's Club Banana Pudding | Serves 4-6

Our State, August 2006

3 3.4-ounce packages instant vanilla pudding

5 cups milk

8 ounces sour cream

1 12-ounce box vanilla wafers

9 ounces frozen whipped topping, thawed

5 or 6 large bananas, sliced

Mix pudding with milk (by hand) until it thickens. Add sour cream; add half of whipped topping. Layer vanilla wafers, bananas, and pudding mixture until all used, ending with pudding. Top with remaining half of whipped topping. Chill until firm or overnight.

— The Rock Barn Club of Golf *cookbook, now out of print, produced by the Rock Barn Women's Club of Conover.*

Dawn Scott's Banana Pudding | Serves 4-6

Our State, November 2009

¾ cup sugar (you can use as little as ¼ cup)

¼ cup flour

¼ tsp. salt (optional)

2 eggs, separated

2 cups milk

1 tsp. vanilla extract

3 bananas

1 box of your favorite vanilla wafers (fat-free wafers don't work as well)

¼ cup sugar (sugar substitutes can be used)

About this recipe:
Cookbook author and Wake County resident Foy Allen Edelman uncovered many great bakers for *Our State*'s November 2009 issue, including Burlington resident Dawn Scott, who shared her recipe for banana pudding. "This recipe is from my grandmother, and she grew up in Caswell County," Scott explains. "When my mother was in nursing school [at Rex Hospital] in the '40s, she couldn't graduate and get her RN degree without being able to make a lump-free custard. That's how important it was in that day."

Pour milk into a double boiler. Heat until scalded. Use a glass measuring cup to mix the flour and sugar. Beat the egg yolks slightly; then gradually add them to the hot milk, stirring constantly.

When the yolks are absorbed into the hot milk, begin pouring small amounts of the hot milk and egg yolks into the sugar and flour. Remember to continue stirring so that no lumps develop as the two mixtures blend.

Slowly pour the thick mixture back into the double boiler. Keep stirring and cooking for about 15 minutes until the mixture becomes a custard. This may take a little longer, depending on how thick you like the custard.

When the custard has reached desired consistency, remove from heat and let cool. Continue stirring as the custard cools so that a thick film does not form on top. When cool, add the vanilla. Peel and slice the bananas. In an oven-safe dish, alternately layer the vanilla wafers, banana slices, and custard.

Preheat oven to 400°. Beat the egg whites until stiff. Add ¼ cup of sugar, and beat a few more minutes. Then pour meringue over the top of the pudding, being sure to spread it out to the edges. Bake until the meringue peaks are golden brown, about 5 to 7 minutes.

Easy Banana Pudding | Serves 8-10

Our State, March 1990

- 2 boxes (6-serving size) instant vanilla pudding
- 5 cups cold milk
- 1 cup sour cream
- 1 carton (9 ounces) whipped topping
- 1 box (1 pound) vanilla wafers
- Sliced bananas

Beat pudding mix with milk until thick. Blend in sour cream and whipped topping. Spread a layer of vanilla wafers in a deep bowl. Add a layer of bananas, then a layer of pudding. Repeat layers until all pudding is used, then top with a few vanilla wafers for garnish. Refrigerate, covered, for several hours until thoroughly chilled.
Makes 8 to 10 servings.

A reader request for an easy banana pudding brought in this recipe, courtesy of Mary Debruhl of Goldsboro, who credits Lucille Turnage of La Grange.

Cheerwine Cake | page 14

Cake

Cheerwine Cake
Tub Jelly Cake
Pineapple Refrigerator Cake
1-2-3 Cake
Spicy Apple Cake
Apple Stack Cake
Fig Cake
Ocracoke Fig Cake
Italian Love Cake
Southern Light Fruitcake
Mother's Fruitcake
Three-Step Layer Cake
Quick Cupcakes
Pink Lemonade Cupcakes
Carrot Cupcakes
Double Chocolate Cupcakes
Coconut Pound Cake
Daddy's Pound Cake
Grandma Gloria's Pound Cake
Five Flavor Pound Cake
Sour Cream Pound Cake
Cream Cheese Pound Cake
Crunchy Pound Cake
Low-Fat Peach Pound Cake
Black Walnut Pound Cake
Lemon Pound Cake
Light Chocolate Pound Cake

Cheerwine Cake

Our State, August 2004

For the cake:

1 cup Cheerwine

1 box devil's food cake mix

1 tsp. almond extract

For the frosting:

⅓ cup Cheerwine

½ cup margarine

¼ cup cocoa

2½ cups powdered sugar

¼ tsp. almond extract

1 cup nuts, chopped

Heat oven to 350°. Grease and flour a 13-x-9-inch baking pan. To make cake, prepare cake mix as directed on box, except substitute 1 cup Cheerwine for the water. Add almond extract. Pour into cake pan, and bake as directed.

To make frosting, heat Cheerwine, margarine, and cocoa to boiling. Pour over powdered sugar in a large bowl and blend until smooth. Stir in almond extract. Mix in nuts. Cool until lukewarm, about 20 minutes. As soon as cake is done, pour frosting over hot cake.

Developed in Salisbury in 1917, the North Carolina-created beverage is right at home as the secret ingredient in a chocolate cake.

Tub Jelly Cake

Our State, December 2005

1 box Moist Supreme Yellow Cake Mix with Double Pudding (18.25 oz.)

1 large jar (32 oz.) thick apple jelly

1 small jar (12 oz.) red currant jelly or red raspberry jelly

Shredded coconut

Prepare cake mix according to instructions on box. Bake in round layer cake pans. Pour small quantity of batter into pan to yield a thin layer, a little thicker than a pancake. Set layers aside to cool. Mix currant and apple jellies, and refrigerate. To assemble cake, stack layers with jelly between each layer. Jelly should also cover top of cake. Sprinkle the top layer with shredded coconut.

Eastern North Carolina lore has it that this old-time Carteret County staple may have evolved from a local merchant who sold scoops of jelly from a large tub in his store.

Pineapple Refrigerator Cake

The State, February 1992

- 2 sticks butter, softened
- 1½ cups sugar
- 2 eggs, lightly beaten
- 1 can crushed pineapple
- 1 box (14 oz. vanilla wafers, crushed,
- 1 cup chopped nuts
- Vanilla ice cream (optional)
- Maraschino cherries (optional)

Beat butter with sugar until light and fluffy. Beat in eggs. Drain pineapple; reserve juice. Stir pineapple into butter mixture. Stir in enough pineapple juice to make butter mixture easy to spread. Refrigerate remaining juice to use at another time. (Stir into orange juice for a refreshing flavor.) Spread about ⅓ crushed wafers evenly in a greased, paper-lined 9-inch square pan, spreading evenly. Spread crumbs with half of pineapple mixture. Sprinke half of nuts evenly over top. Sprinkle half of remaining wafer crumbs over nuts, then remaining pineapple mixture and remaining nuts. Sprinkle last of wafer crumbs evenly over top. Press lightly to set layers. Refrigerate at least 12 hours before cutting into squares. When serving, top each square with a dip of vanilla ice cream and a cherry, if desired.

Edie Low of Rock Hill, South Carolina, wrote Our State*'s "Tar Heel Recipes" column throughout the 1980s, '90s, and 2000s.*

1-2-3 Cake

Our State, April 1997

- 1 cup butter
- 2 cups sugar
- 3 cups all-purpose flour
- 2 tsp. baking powder
- 4 or 5 eggs
- 1 cup milk
- 1 tsp. vanilla

Cream butter and sugar well. Sift flour with baking powder. Beat eggs well. Add eggs to butter and sugar.

Alternately add flour and milk, then vanilla. Pour batter into three cake pans that have been greased and floured. Bake at 375°. (Length of baking time was not given; test frequently after 25 minutes so cake does not overcook.)

— Recipe submitted by Mary Moss Darden of Virginia Beach, Virginia, who credits her grandmother, Annie Harrell Stewart, of Charlotte

Spicy Apple Cake | Makes one 9-inch-round cake

Our State, October 2005

- 1½ cups unsifted cake flour
- 1 tsp. baking powder
- ½ tsp. baking soda
- ¼ tsp. salt
- ½ tsp. ground cinnamon
- ½ tsp. freshly grated nutmeg
- ¼ tsp. ground allspice
- ¼ tsp. ground ginger
- ⅛ tsp. ground cloves
- ½ cup unsalted butter, softened
- ¾ cup granulated sugar
- 3 Tbsp. firmly packed light brown sugar
- 1 extra-large egg plus two extra-large egg yolks, at room temperature
- ¼ cup milk blended with 2 tsp. vanilla extract, at room temperature
- 1½ cups peeled, cored, and shredded tart cooking apples
- confectioners' sugar for dusting

Lightly butter and flour a 9-inch-round springform pan; set aside. Preheat the oven to 350°.

Sift the flour with the baking powder, baking soda, salt, cinnamon, nutmeg, allspice, ginger, and cloves onto a large sheet of waxed paper. Cream the butter in the large bowl of an electric mixer on moderately high speed for 1 minute. Beat in the granulated sugar and brown sugar, and continue beating for 2 minutes. Beat in the egg. Beat in the egg yolks. Blend in the milk-vanilla mixture, and beat for 1 minute. With the mixer on low speed, add the sifted flour mixture in 2 additions, beating until the particles of flour from the first portion have been absorbed before adding the next. By hand, fold in the shredded apples. Spoon the batter into the prepared pan. Using a small spatula, push about ½-inch of batter up the sides of the baking pan to keep the batter level as it rises and bakes.

Bake the cake on the lower-third-level rack of the preheated oven for about 40 to 45 minutes or until a wooden pick inserted in the center of the cake comes out clean and dry. The cake will pull away slightly from the edges of the pan when done.

Let cool in the pan on a wire rack for 10 minutes, then remove the hinged ring of the pan. Let cool completely. Dust the top of the cake with a little confectioners' sugar.

A Country Baking Treasury, *HarperCollins, helped us out with a good use for the extra Winesap, Rome, and Stayman apples you may have lying around.*

Apple Stack Cake | Serves 10-12

Our State, November 2009

Apple Filling:

1 pound dried apples

1 tsp. cinnamon

1 cup sugar

½ tsp. salt

Cakes:

4 to 5 cups self-rising flour

1 tsp. baking soda

2 tsp. ginger

1 tsp. cinnamon and cloves, to taste

½ cup shortening

½ cup sugar

1 cup molasses

2 eggs

½ cup buttermilk

1 Tbsp. vanilla extract

About this recipe:
Charity Ray of Mars Hill has been making her Apple Stack Cake for years. *Our State*'s contributor, Foy Allen Edelman, discovered Ray's tasty creation and shared the favored family recipe with us. "We had a fruit orchard in the backyard when we were young," says Ray. "We dried our apples outside in the sun. ... They're better when they're dried outside."

Apple Filling

This mixture makes a juicy, applesauce-type filling. Begin the filling the night before you plan to make the cakes. Soak the dried apples overnight in enough water to cover. The next day, cook them on low heat until tender. Mash until smooth, and add 1 tsp. of cinnamon, 1 cup of sugar, and ½ tsp. of salt. Put the mixture back on the heat, and bring to a boil, being careful not to scorch. When the sugar dissolves and the mixture thickens, remove from heat and let cool.

Cakes

Preheat oven to 350°. Lightly grease 8 round cake pans. Combine flour, baking soda, ginger, cinnamon, and cloves; set aside. Cream shortening and sugar until the mixture is light and fluffy. Blend in the molasses. Add eggs, beating well. Add dry ingredients to the creamed mixture in thirds, alternating with buttermilk and beating well after each addition. Add the vanilla last. The dough will be very stiff and have the consistency of cornbread. Place the dough on a well-floured surface, working in enough flour to make it easy to handle. Divide into 8 balls. Roll each one out as a large cookie, about 6 inches in diameter, and press into prepared cake pans. Bake the cakes for 12-15 minutes, or until lightly browned. Remove cakes from the oven and allow to cool.

When the cakes have cooled, put a cake layer on a plate and spread the top of it with some of the apple filling. Add more layers, and put filling in between each one. Build it into a stack. Put filling on the sides to help keep the cake moist. Cover and refrigerate.

Fig Cake | Serves 8-10

Our State, June 2007

1 cup self-rising flour

1 cup sugar

Pinch salt

½ cup milk

½ cup melted butter

½ tsp. vanilla

2 eggs

1 pint figs, mashed

Combine flour, sugar, and salt.
Add milk and melted butter, vanilla, eggs, and mashed figs. Mix well. Pour into an 8-x-8-inch pan. Bake at 350° for 30 to 40 minutes. Test. Cut in squares while still in pan.

— Roanoke Island Roots, A Collection of Roanoke Island History, Memories, and Daniels' Family Recipes *by Brenda Daniels Harrison. Calico Kitchen Press, 1991.*

Ocracoke Fig Cake

Our State, November 2009

1 cup salad oil

1½ cup sugar

3 eggs

1 tsp. soda, dissolved in hot water

2 cups flour

1 tsp. nutmeg

1 tsp. allspice

1 tsp. cinnamon

1 tsp. salt

¼ cup buttermilk

1 tsp. vanilla

1 cup preserved figs, chopped

1 cup chopped nuts

Beat 3 eggs; add sugar and oil. After sifting dry ingredients, add to egg mixture alternately with buttermilk. Add vanilla, and fold in figs and nuts. Pour into greased, oblong pan and bake at 325° for 45 minutes to 1 hour, or in a well-greased tube pan at 350° just a little longer.

Outer Banks dwellers developed their own cherished regional recipes from the proliferation of local fruit, like the figs that have been growing on Ocracoke Island since the 1700s.

Along with our story on Ocracoke's famous figs, we published this treasured recipe courtesy of The Ocracoke Cook Book.

Italian Love Cake

Our State, February 1999

- 1 package marble cake mix
- 2 pounds ricotta cheese, drained
- ¾ cup sugar
- 3 eggs
- 1 tsp. vanilla
- 1 cup milk
- 1 package (4-serving) chocolate instant pudding mix
- 1 container (8 ounces) frozen whipped topping

Prepare cake mix as directed; turn batter into an ungreased 15-x-21-inch glass baking dish. Beat together the ricotta, sugar, eggs, and vanilla. Spoon mixture evenly over cake batter. Bake at 350° for 1 hour. Cheese mixture will sink to bottom of cake while baking. Cool cake on a rack for 2 hours. Meanwhile, blend milk with pudding mix. Refrigerate until chilled. Mix together the pudding and thawed whipped topping. Use mixture to frost the cake. Refrigerate until ready to serve.

Edie Low of Rock Hill, South Carolina, wrote Our State*'s "Tar Heel Recipes" column throughout the 1980s, '90s, and 2000s.*

Pumpkin Layer Cake | Serves 8

Our State, November 2006

- 2½ cups all-purpose flour
- 1 tsp. baking soda
- 1 tsp. baking powder
- ½ tsp. salt
- 1 tsp. ground cloves
- 1 tsp. cinnamon
- 2 cups sugar
- 6 eggs, beaten
- 2½ cups mashed pumpkin
- 1 cup chopped walnuts

Preheat oven to 350°. Sift together the flour, baking soda, baking powder, salt, cloves, and cinnamon. Put the sugar and eggs in another bowl, and beat until fluffy. Add the pumpkin, and stir to mix. Mix in the flour mixture. Dust the walnuts with a little flour, and stir in. Pour into three 8-inch greased and floured cake pans. Bake for 15 minutes. Cool and ice with chocolate frosting.

Instead of traditional pumpkin pie, consider serving a pumpkin layer cake, courtesy of Mama Dip's Family Cookbook *by Mildred Council, UNC Press, Chapel Hill. 2005.*

Southern Light Fruitcake

Our State, December 1996

- 4 cups pecan halves
- 2 cups walnut halves
- 2 cups whole candied cherries
- 2 cups diced candied pineapple
- 1½ cups light raisins
- 3 cups sifted all-purpose flour, divided
- 1½ cups butter
- 1½ cups sugar
- 3 large eggs
- 3 Tbsp. plus 1 tsp. lemon extract
- 1 tsp. baking powder
- Red and green cherries for garnish

Combine pecans, walnuts, cherries, pineapple, and raisins. Toss with one cup flour and set aside.

Cream butter with sugar until light and fluffy. Add eggs, one at a time, beating well after each addition. Stir in lemon extract. Sift remaining two cups of flour with baking powder. Add in thirds to creamed mixture, blending well. Add batter to nut-fruit mixture, mixing well. Batter will be stiff. Spoon mixture into well-greased, 10-inch tube pan.

Cover tightly with foil. Place a pan of hot water on bottom oven rack. Place cake on rack above water. Bake at 300° for 2½ hours. Remove foil; bake five to seven minutes longer, until top is light brown. Cool completely, then remove from pan. Garnish cake with poinsettias cut from the red and green cherries. Store cake in a tightly covered container.

In 1996, Nancy Wilson of Kenansville sent us this recipe that she and her mother, Henrietta Grady, baked each December beginning in the early 1960s.

Mother's Fruitcake

Our State, December 2005

1 pound butter

1 pound brown sugar

12 egg yolks

1 cup molasses

12 egg whites

4 cups flour

4 tsp. allspice

4 tsp. cinnamon

1 tsp. nutmeg

1½ tsp. mace

2 pounds Sultana raisins

1 pound currants

1½ pounds preserved lemon rinds

1½ pounds orange rind

1 pound candied cherries

1 pound candied pineapple

1½ pounds citron

2 cups preserved figs

1 cup chopped pecans

1 cup fruit juice

¼ tsp. soda dissolved in 1 Tbsp. hot water

Line 5 or 6 large loaf pans with brown paper, and grease well. Set aside. Cream together the butter and brown sugar until thoroughly blended. Add beaten egg yolks and molasses, and beat well. Fold in stiffly beaten egg whites.

Set aside 1 cup of flour; sift together remaining flour and spices. Add the flour mixture to egg mixture. Mix prepared fruits, and dredge with the 1 cup of flour. Add figs, pecans, and juice to the mixture, and mix all together well.

Last, add soda dissolved in hot water. Fill loaf pans about half full.

Bake in a slow oven: 275° for three or four hours for large pans, or 325° for small pans.

— From Christmas Kin/Seasonal Keepsakes from "The Mailboat," *a newsletter containing articles about Outer Banks communities. This recipe belonged to Lena Williams of Ocracoke and was related by her daughter, Belle Brown.*

Three-Step Layer Cake | Serves 10-12

Our State, September 1996

Step 1 - Sift together:

2¼ cups sifted cake flour

1½ cups sugar

2½ tsp. baking powder

1 tsp. of salt

Step 2 - Cut in:

½ cup vegetable shortening

1 tsp. vanilla extract

⅔ cup milk

Step 3 — Beat 2 minutes, then add:

⅓ cup milk

2 eggs

Beat two minutes, then turn batter into greased and floured layer pans. Bake at 350° for 35 to 40 minutes, until layers test done. Remove pans to a rack to cool for 10 minutes. Turn out, and ice as desired.

Edie Low of Rock Hill, South Carolina, wrote and compiled Our State*'s "Tar Heel Recipes" column throughout the 1980s, '90s, and 2000s.*

Quick Cupcakes | Makes 18 cupcakes

The State, May 1993

1½ cups sifted all-purpose flour

¾ cup sugar

¼ cup dry cocoa

1 tsp. baking soda

½ tsp. salt

1 cup water

¼ cup vegetable oil

1 Tbsp. vinegar

1 tsp. vanilla extract

Combine and blend well the flour, sugar, cocoa, baking soda, and salt. Stir in the water, oil, vinegar, and vanilla. Beat with a whisk just until batter is smooth. Ladle batter into paper-lined muffin cups, filling each ⅔ full. Bake at 375° for 16 to 18 minutes, or until the cupcakes test is done. (A toothpick inserted in the center will come out clean.) Cool 10 minutes, then remove to a rack to cool completely. Ice and use immediately, or store, unfrosted, in airtight containers in a freezer up to two months. Thaw completely before frosting.

— Marcie Greenleaf, Greensboro

Pink Lemonade Cupcakes with Coconut and Quick Butter Frosting | 12 cupcakes

Our State, February 2009

For cupcakes:

3 large eggs, separated

1 cup granulated sugar

4 Tbsp. unsalted butter, melted

¾ cup milk

grated zest and juice of 1 lemon

1 tsp. vanilla extract

1½ cups all-purpose flour

1½ tsp. baking powder

pinch of salt

For frosting:

1½ sticks unsalted butter, softened

2 cups powdered sugar, sifted

juice of one lemon

1½ tsp. vanilla extract

3 drops red food coloring

For Garnish:

½ cup sweetened coconut flakes

Preheat oven to 350°. Line a 12-cup muffin pan with paper liners. In the bowl of an electric mixer fitted with the paddle attachment, beat egg yolks and sugar together until pale yellow. Add melted butter, milk, lemon zest and juice, and vanilla; mix until smooth. Add flour, baking powder, and salt, and mix until just combined; set aside. In a separate large bowl, whisk egg whites until soft peaks form. Fold whipped egg whites into batter to combine. Fill muffin cups, and bake for 20 to 25 minutes or until fully cooked.

When the cupcakes are cool, prepare frosting. In the bowl of an electric mixer fitted with the paddle attachment, beat softened butter, powdered sugar, lemon juice, and vanilla together until smooth. Add red food coloring, and mix until frosting turns a pale pink.

Smooth frosting onto cupcakes, and garnish with coconut.

Food stylist and recipe writer Charlotte Fekete began writing Our State*'s "Carolina Kitchen" column in 2008.*

Carrot Cupcakes with Orange Cream Cheese Frosting | Makes 12 cupcakes

Our State, February 2009

For cupcakes:
1 stick unsalted butter, melted

1 cup light brown sugar

3 large eggs

¼ cup milk

1 tsp. vanilla extract

4 medium carrots, peeled and grated coarsely with a box grater

1½ cups all-purpose flour

1½ tsp. baking powder

1 tsp. ground cinnamon

pinch of salt

For frosting:
6 ounces cream cheese, softened

6 Tbsp. unsalted butter, softened

1 cup powdered sugar, sifted

grated zest and juice of one orange

Preheat oven to 350°. Line a 12-cup muffin pan with paper liners. In a large bowl, mix together butter and brown sugar. Add eggs, milk, vanilla, and grated carrots; stir to combine. Gently stir in flour, baking powder, cinnamon, and salt until just combined. Fill muffin cups, and bake for 20 to 25 minutes or until fully cooked.

Once cupcakes are cool, prepare frosting. In the bowl of an electric mixer fitted with the paddle attachment, beat cream cheese, softened butter, powdered sugar, and orange zest and juice until smooth. Spread a generous amount onto each cupcake before serving.

— Charlotte Fekete, Birmingham, Alabama

Double Chocolate Cupcakes with Sour Cream Frosting | Makes 12 cupcakes

Our State, February 2009

For cupcakes:

- 1 stick unsalted butter
- ½ cup semisweet chocolate chips
- 1 cup granulated sugar
- 1 cup sour cream
- ⅓ cup milk
- 2 large eggs
- ½ tsp. vanilla extract
- ¾ cup all-purpose flour
- ¼ cup cocoa powder
- ½ tsp. baking powder
- pinch of salt

For frosting:

- ½ cup sour cream
- ½ cup powdered sugar, sifted
- 1½ Tbsp. cocoa powder

Preheat oven to 350°. Line a 12-cup muffin pan with paper liners. Place butter and chocolate chips into a large bowl, and microwave on high for 30 seconds. Stir and microwave again for 30 seconds to melt butter and chocolate completely. Remove bowl from microwave, and stir in sugar, sour cream, milk, eggs, and vanilla. Whisk in flour, cocoa, baking powder, and salt, and mix until completely combined. Fill lined muffin cups, and bake for 20 to 25 minutes or until fully cooked.

Once cupcakes are cool, prepare frosting. In a medium bowl, stir together sour cream, powdered sugar, and cocoa until completely combined and smooth onto cupcakes.

— Charlotte Fekete, Birmingham, Alabama

Coconut Pound Cake

Coconut Pound Cake

Our State, January 2007

2 cups sugar

1 cup vegetable shortening

5 eggs, allowed to come to room temperature

2 cups flour

1½ tsp. baking powder

1 tsp. salt

1 cup buttermilk

1½ tsp. coconut flavoring

1 cup flaked coconut

Grease and flour a 10-inch tube pan. Preheat oven to 350°. Using an electric mixer, cream together sugar and vegetable shortening until well blended. Add eggs, one at a time, beating well after each addition. Combine flour, baking powder, and salt.
Add this mixture to the sugar mixture, a little at a time, alternately with the buttermilk, beginning and ending with flour. Add coconut flavoring. Stir to blend. Stir in coconut.

Bake in oven 50 minutes, or until a toothpick comes out clean.

— Dorothy Farr, Louisville, Kentucky.

Daddy's Pound Cake

Our State, September 2003

1 stick butter

1 cup Crisco

3 cups sugar

5 eggs

1 tsp. baking powder

3 cups flour

1 cup milk

1 tsp. vanilla extract

1 tsp. lemon extract

Cream butter, Crisco, and sugar. Add eggs one at a time; beat after each. Add flour and milk alternately. Add baking powder, vanilla, and lemon flavoring. Let lemon run over a little. Bake at 350° for an hour and five minutes.

In a story on classic pound cakes, Virginia Clinard shared with us her recipe, which won second place in the Judge's Favorite Category at the Fine Art of Being Southern Symposium at Wingate University in 2001.

Grandma Gloria's Pound Cake

Our State, January 2007

2 sticks butter

½ cup vegetable shortening

3 cups sugar

5 eggs, allowed to come to room temperature

3 cups plain flour

1 cup whole milk

½ tsp. baking powder

½ tsp. salt

2 Tbsp. pure vanilla extract

1 Tbsp. lemon extract

Let butter soften really well, then cream the butter, shortening, and sugar. Add eggs, one at a time, beating each well, into the creamed mixture. Add flour, 1 cup at a time, alternating with ⅓ cup of milk. Mix each portion in well. Add baking powder and salt, vanilla extract and lemon extract, and beat well. Pour mixture into a 10-inch, greased and floured tube pan, smoothing to the sides with a spatula. "Pound" the pan on the counter a few times to settle any air bubbles (by lifting pan about 2 inches and dropping onto counter).

Place in cold oven. Turn the oven to 325° and bake for 90 minutes.

Pound cake recipes have been popular in Our State *magazine for decades; Gloria Hemmerle of Rocky Mount submitted this one, which gets its start in a cold oven.*

Five Flavor Pound Cake

Our State, August 2001

3 cups cake flour, sifted

3 cups sugar

1 tsp. salt

1½ cups butter

1 cup milk

1 tsp. vanilla extract

1 tsp. lemon extract

1 tsp. almond extract

1 tsp. coconut extract

1 tsp. rum extract

Cream butter, add sugar. Add eggs, one at a time, and cream well. Sift flour and salt together. Add flour mixture and milk. Add extracts. Pour in greased and floured Bundt or tube pan. Bake at 325° for 1 ½ hours.

Our State*'s former "Carolina Kitchen" columnist Erica Derr contributed recipes to the magazine from 2000-2008.*

Sour Cream Pound Cake from Dottie Knight | Serves about 24

Our State, September 2003

2 sticks butter

3 cups sugar

6 eggs

1 cup sour cream

3 cups cake flour

¼ tsp baking powder

2 Tbsp. lemon or vanilla extract

Glaze:

½-¾ cups confectioners' sugar

3-4 Tbsp. lemon juice

Cream together butter and sugar. Add eggs, beating in one at a time; then add sour cream. Then add 3 cups cake flour, baking powder, and lemon or vanilla extract. Beat just until well blended. Pour into greased and floured tube pan.
Bake in preheated 325° oven for 1½ hours. About five minutes before cake is done, prepare lemon glaze. Bring to a boil and cook, stirring constantly, for about one minute, ½ to ¾ cups powdered sugar and 3 or 4 Tbsp. of lemon juice. Pour glaze over hot cake when it's done.

Our State *writer Anne Barnhill says, "When Dottie Love Knight passed from this world, she left a wonderful gift for her family and friends. Printed inside the funeral service program was the handwritten recipe for her special Sour Cream Pound Cake."*

Cream Cheese Pound Cake

Our State, August 2001

8-ounce package cream cheese, softened

3 sticks butter, softened

3 cups sugar

6 eggs

3 cups sifted cake flour

¼ tsp. salt

1 tsp. vanilla

Preheat oven to 325°. Combine cream cheese, butter, and sugar, beating until light and fluffy. Add eggs, one at a time, beating well after each addition. Blend in flour, salt, and vanilla. Do not beat. Pour in greased Bundt or tube pan. Bake from 1 hour and 15 minutes to 1½ hours, until a tester comes out clean.

Cool in pan for 10 minutes before turning out on a rack to cool. Dust with powdered sugar and garnish with lemon, if desired.

— Erica Derr, Greensboro

Crunchy Pound Cake

Our State, August 1998

1 cup shortening

2 cups sugar

6 medium eggs

1 tsp. lemon extract

1 tsp. vanilla extract

2 cups cake flour

Cream shortening and sugar together with an electric mixer at medium speed. Stir in eggs, one at a time, beating well after each addition. Add lemon and vanilla extracts. Sift flour three times, then add to creamed mixture ⅓ at a time. Place batter in a buttered tube pan or two loaf pans. Start in a cold oven, and bake one hour at 300°.

Jane Whetzel of Wilmington responded to a reader question of how to make a pound cake with a crunchy top. Whetzel also says this recipe makes its own icing.

Low-Fat Peach Pound Cake

Our State, July 1999

Vegetable cooking spray

1 ½ cups sugar, divided

½ cup plain low-fat yogurt

⅓ cup vegetable oil

3 eggs

2 egg whites

1 tsp. vanilla

3 cups flour, divided

1 ½ tsp. baking powder

½ tsp. salt

2 cups chopped, fresh peaches

Spray a 10-inch tube pan with cooking spray. Sprinkle with 1 tsp. sugar. Combine oil and yogurt; gradually add remaining sugar, beating well. Add whole eggs and whites, one at a time, beating well after each addition. Add vanilla and mix well. Combine 2¾ cups flour, baking powder, and salt. Gradually add to yogurt mixture; beat until well blended. Dredge peaches with remaining ¼ cup flour. Fold peaches into batter. Pour batter into prepared pan. Bake at 350° for 1 hour, 10 minutes. Remove from pan and cool completely.

The North Carolina Department of Agriculture and Consumer Services knows how to make good use of mountain-grown or Sandhills-area peaches.

Black Walnut Pound Cake | Makes about 20 servings

Our State, May 1999

For cake

1 cup butter-flavored shortening

1 stick butter, softened

3 cups sugar

6 eggs at room temperature

3 cups all-purpose flour

1 tsp. baking powder

2 tsp. black walnut flavoring

1 cup milk

1 cup chopped black walnuts

For Penuche frosting

½ cup butter

1 cup brown sugar, packed

¼ cup milk

2 cups confectioners' sugar

1 tsp. vanilla

½ cup chopped black walnuts

Cream together the shortening, butter, and sugar. Beat in eggs, one at a time, until the yellow disappears. Sift together the flour and baking powder. Stir walnut flavoring into milk. Toss nuts with 2 Tbsp. of flour. Add flour and milk alternately to butter mixture, beginning and ending with flour. When batter is well blended, fold in walnuts. Turn batter into a greased, floured 2-inch tube pan. Bake 1½ hours at 325°, or until a toothpick inserted in the center comes out clean. Remove from pan, and let cool. Frost, if desired, with penuche frosting.

For Penuche Frosting

Melt butter in a medium pan. Add brown sugar; boil 2 minutes. Stir in milk, bring to a boil, and remove from heat. Cool to lukewarm. Beat in confectioners' sugar and vanilla. Stir in walnuts. Frost cake. Makes about 20 servings.

— Nancy Wilson, Kenansville

Lemon Pound Cake

Our State, April 1993

3 cups all-purpose flour

½ tsp. baking powder

¼ tsp. salt

3 cups sugar

½ cup butter-flavored solid shortening

½ cup solid vegetable shortening

5 eggs

1 cup milk

¼ cup sour cream

2 Tbsp. lemon juice

1 tsp. vanilla

¼ cup poppy seeds

Glaze and Topping

½ cup graham cracker crumbs

¼ cup firmly packed brown sugar

¼ cup chopped walnuts

½ tsp. ground cinnamon

3 Tbsp. butter-flavored solid shortening

¾ cup confectioners' sugar

½ tsp. grated lemon peel

1 Tbsp. lemon juice

Lemon slices for garnish (optional)

To make cake, sift flour with baking powder and salt. Beat sugar with the two shortenings until well-blended.

Beat in eggs, one at a time. Add flour alternately with milk, beating at low speed after each addition just until mixed. Blend in sour cream, lemon juice, and vanilla.

Stir in poppy seeds, using a spoon. Spoon batter into a greased and floured 10-inch Bundt pan. Smooth surface of batter and tap pan on countertop so no bubbles are in the batter.

Bake at 325° for 1 hour and 30 minutes, or until a toothpick inserted in the center comes out clean. Cool five minutes before removing from pan. Turn cake out, top side down, onto a rack; cool completely. Transfer to a cake plate.

Meanwhile, combine graham cracker crumbs with brown sugar, walnuts, cinnamon, and shortening. Stir until blended and crumbly. Set aside.

Combine confectioners' sugar with lemon peel and lemon juice in a small bowl. Stir to blend, then drizzle mixture over cooked cake in a zigzag pattern. Before glaze has time to harden, sprinkle quickly with graham cracker mixture.

Decorate around base of cake with lemon slices, if desired.

Pam Walsh of Thomasville won a place in the regional bake-off of a statewide cooking contest in 1993 with this recipe featuring a crunchy glaze.

Light Chocolate Pound Cake

Our State, January 2007

1 stick margarine or butter

½ cup + 1 Tbsp. vegetable shortening

3 cups sugar

5 eggs

1 cup milk

3 cups plain flour

½ tsp. salt

½ tsp. baking powder

4 Tbsp. cocoa

1 Tbsp. vanilla extract

Cream margarine or butter, shortening, and sugar together. Add eggs one at a time, beating well after each addition. Sift flour, baking powder, salt, and cocoa together, then add alternately with milk. Stir in the vanilla extract.

Grease a 10-inch tube pan very well, then sprinkle some sugar in the cake pan before pouring batter in to create a faux frosting, if desired.

Bake for 1 hour and 20 minutes at 350° or until a cake tester comes out clean.

— Alice Bowman of Taylorsville

Dixie Peanut Brittle | page 36

Candy

Dixie Peanut Brittle

Seafoam

Peanut Butter Fondue

Wife-Catching
Chocolate Fondue

Carolina Cranachan

Buttermints

Creamy Potato Fudge

Christmas Fudge

Dixie Peanut Brittle | Makes about 2 pounds

Our State, May 2002

- 2 cups granulated sugar
- 1 cup light corn syrup
- ½ cup water
- ½ tsp. salt
- 3 cups raw shelled peanuts, skins on
- 2 Tbsp. butter
- 2 tsp. baking soda

Heat sugar, syrup, water, and salt to a rolling boil in a heavy saucepan. Add peanuts. Reduce heat to medium and stir constantly. Cook to hard crack stage (293° to 300° F.). Add butter, then baking soda. Beat rapidly, and pour on a buttered surface, spreading to ¼-inch thickness. When cool, break into pieces. Store in an airtight container.

In business since 1919, Bertie County Peanuts has had plenty of experience in making brittle from the out-of-hand snack. We're happy to share their famous recipe.

Seafoam

Our State, December 2000

- 2 cups brown sugar
- ½ cup water
- 1 egg white
- 1 tsp. vanilla
- ½ cup chopped nuts

Combine brown sugar and water, and boil until soft ball or 239° on candy thermometer. Beat egg white until very stiff; add sugar syrup slowly and lightly to egg white. Put in vanilla and chopped nuts. Drop by spoonfuls on waxed paper.

Our State *writer Martha Long contributed her cousin's recipe for seafoam, which, she says, came from an old Rumford baking powder cookbook.*

Peanut Butter Fondue | Makes about 1¾ cups

Our State, September 1993

- 1 cup peanut butter
- ½ cup evaporated milk
- ½ cup brown sugar
- 2 Tbsp. butter
- Dash of salt

In a fondue pot or heavy saucepan, combine peanut butter, milk, sugar, butter, and salt, blending well. Cook over low heat until hot, stirring constantly. Serve as a dip with fruit, crackers, etc.

Edie Low of Rock Hill, South Carolina, wrote Our State*'s "Tar Heel Recipes" column throughout the 1980s, '90s, and 2000s.*

Wife-Catching Chocolate Fondue | Serves 4

Our State, January 2004

- 4 3-ounce bars Toblerone chocolate with honey and nuts
- 1 cup heavy cream
- 3 Tbsp. Kahlua (optional)

Break the chocolate into pieces and place in a heavy saucepan. Add cream, and stir over low heat until the chocolate is melted and the mixture is smooth. Transfer to a fondue pot over medium heat, being careful not to let the chocolate boil. Stir in Kahlua just before serving, if desired. Serve with marshmallows, squares of pound cake, ladyfingers, strawberries, bananas, etc.

Our State*'s former "Carolina Kitchen" columnist Erica Derr contributed recipes to the magazine from 2000-2008.*

Carolina Cranachan | Serves 4

Our State, July 2006

- ½ cup coarse-cut (or "steel-cut") oats
- 1 cup heavy cream ("double" cream or Devonshire cream, if you can find it)
- 1 tsp. of local honey
- 1 Tbsp. confectioners' sugar
- ½ tsp. vanilla extract
- 1 Tbsp. whiskey (optional)
- 1 cup fresh blueberries, picked free of stems, rinsed, and gently patted dry
- 4 fresh mint leaves (for garnish, optional)
- 4 shortbread cookies

Preheat oven to 350°. Spread oats in a thin layer on a baking sheet. Toast in the oven for about 10 minutes or until nicely browned. Set aside to cool.

In a medium bowl, whip the cream to firm peaks. Gently fold in the honey, confectioners' sugar, vanilla, toasted oats, and whiskey, if desired. Divide the berries among four large wine goblets or other dessert dishes. Top with cranachan cream. Garnish with mint leaf, and serve with a shortbread cookie on the side.

Cranachan is a traditional Scottish dessert that can also be made with other berries. The honey typically used is a thick heather blossom honey, but North Carolina local honey does just fine.

Hand-pulled Buttermints

Our State, December 2009

After seeing a lady in Roxboro make buttermints when she was a child, Nita Whitfield of Durham developed her own recipe and has won five first-place ribbons and one second-place ribbon for her mints at the North Carolina State Fair. Here, Whitfield takes us through the 17 steps to create the prize-winning confection.

3 cups Dixie Crystals sugar

1 stick butter

1 cup water

6-8 drops pure peppermint oil (lorannoils.com)

Food color, (gel-type, such as Wilton's)

Professional Candy Thermometer (Wilton's Brand)

3 Qt. Revere Ware pot

Marble (14x26x1 inch thick, polished and sealed)

Rubber Spatula (high-heat resistant)

Metal old-fashioned spatula

Scissors (no teeth)

Metal tin to store mints

Wax paper

1. Place pot on burner. Add water and butter. Turn heat on low and melt.

2. After the mixture dissolves, add sugar and mix well with spoon. No need to stir anymore.

3. Place and clip professional thermometer on side of pot. Do not use cheap glass thermometers. They can break, and they are not calibrated.

4. Turn heat up to approximately medium high. Bring mixture to a full rolling boil. Note: You have to learn to adjust the heat under your pot. You want it just hot enough to bring the candy to a full rolling boil. My unit has numbers from 0 to 10. I start my candy on 9, then after 5 minutes turn it up to 9.5, and then at about 8 minutes, I turn it up to 10.

5. Set a timer for 15 minutes, and watch your time. You never need to cook this candy more than 15 minutes. It will reach the right temperature in about 15 minutes.

6. After the candy cooks about 5 minutes, the mixture will "settle" down in the pot some. It is chemically changing and thickening. At this point I turn my heat up a tad. Watch the thermometer; the temperature is rising.

7. At about 8 to 10 minutes, I turn my heat up to 10. The mixture is thickening and at about 15 minutes, you will reach the desired temp

of hard ball stage, which is 260°. During the last 5 minutes, watch the temperature very closely. Do not be distracted, or you will overcook it!

8. When it reaches this temperature, remove the pot from the unit. Put the thermometer into the sudsy water you have prepared, and with the spatula in hand, pour the hot candy mixture up and down the length of the marble. Clean out the pot quickly with the spatula, and run hot sudsy water into the pot to soak while you finish the mint process.

9. The hot candy will spread out very thin on the marble. The cold marble will cool the candy very fast. Add the peppermint oil with a dropper and a very tiny amount of food color if you want color. They are very pretty with no color at all. Do not make them dark colors, it looks awful.

10. Test the edges of the cooling candy by lifting them slightly with your fingers. The middle of the candy area is still very hot, but the outer edges are getting cool and hardening. Turn all of the outer edges of the candy into the center of the candy area, and smush it down with your fingers and palm of your hands.

11. You want to keep this entire mass of candy cooling consistently on the marble. No hard edges or lumps, etc.

12. You maximize three areas of the marble to cool the candy mixture: the center of the marble first, then the left end of the marble and then the far right end of the marble.

13. After the candy has been at the center of the marble for about 2 minutes, roll it down to the left-hand end of the marble and smush it out to absorb the coldness of the marble on that end. (Keep an old-fashioned metal pancake flipper utensil handy in case candy tries to stick to the marble). Wait about 1 minute for it to cool at the left hand end.

14. Then roll up the candy and move it to the other end of the marble and smush it out. It will be much firmer and cooler now and you will really have to smush it hard to spread it out. Only experience can dictate the right time to pick the candy up from this point to start pulling it.

15. When you first pick up the candy off the marble, squeeze it into an oblong shape, and pull it out just a little bit. Then loop the end furthest away from you (hold it with your right hand) back over the end that you have in your left hand. Don't position the ends evenly; lap them over a

couple of inches. Then twist the entire loop together and pull it out some. Don't get carried away and pull it out too far. Just pull it a little and then loop it over again, and then twist it together and pull it out again. It only takes about 3 to 5 minutes for the candy to get to the right consistency. You can't go too fast or too slow. If you pull it too long, it will mess up. So, timing is everything. The candy gets glossy and harder to pull as it reaches the time to stop pulling it.

16. At a clear spot on your counter (not on top of the marble), pull and twist out the candy into a long rope that looks like a big lasso rope. Cut into 3 or 4 equal segments. Then stretch and twist these pieces out until they are about two feet long. Twisting it makes it pretty, and you can more effectively stretch out the candy if you twist and pull it out into long ropes. With old scissors or OXO brand spring-loaded scissors, snip the candy into half-inch-long pieces.

17. Use candy tins that are wide and flat. Put a layer of wax paper in the bottom of the tin. Place half the mints here. Add one more layer of wax paper and add the other half of the mints. A few may stick together; that is fine, as they will break apart after they cure. Shut the tin and let them cure for at least 12 hours. If not eaten in one week, store in refrigerator.

Creamy Potato Fudge | Makes about 1¼ pounds

Our State, March 1999

3 squares (1 ounce each) unsweetened chocolate

3 Tbsp. butter

⅓ cup mashed, unseasoned potatoes

⅛ tsp. salt

1 tsp. vanilla

1 pound confectioners' sugar, sifted

½ cup chopped nuts

Melt chocolate and butter in top of a double boiler over simmering water. Remove from heat.

Stir in potatoes, salt, and vanilla, blending well. Add sugar and mix thoroughly. Add nuts. Knead mixture until smooth. Press into a buttered 8-inch-square pan. Cool in refrigerator before cutting.

Edie Low of Rock Hill, South Carolina, wrote Our State*'s "Tar Heel Recipes" column throughout the 1980s, '90s, and 2000s.*

Christmas Fudge

Our State, December 2000

2 cups sugar

½ tsp. salt

½ stick butter

1 can (5 oz.) evaporated milk

1 package (12 oz.) semisweet chocolate chips

1 Symphony chocolate bar (7.5 oz.) with almonds and toffee bits

1 jar (7 oz.) marshmallow creme

2 tsp. vanilla extract

2 cups coarsely chopped walnuts or pecans

Heavily butter a 9-x-13-inch baking pan and set aside.

Place the sugar, salt, butter, and evaporated milk in a large, heavy saucepan. Bring to a boil over medium-high heat, stirring constantly. When the mixture comes to a boil, reduce heat to medium. Boil gently for 8 to 9 minutes, stirring frequently to make sure the bottom doesn't scorch. Stir in the chocolate chips, chocolate bar, and marshmallow creme until the mixture is well blended.

Stir in the vanilla extract and nuts. Pour the mixture into the prepared pan. Cool at room temperature for several hours, or until set.

Cut into one-inch squares. Store in an airtight container for up to two weeks.

Our State*'s former "Carolina Kitchen" columnist Erica Derr contributed recipes to the magazine from 2000-2008.*

Cheesecake

Caramel Cheesecake with Praline Sauce | page 44

Caramel Cheesecake with Praline Sauce | Serves 12

Our State, December 1999

Crust

2½ Tbsp. graham cracker crumbs

1 Tbsp. sugar

Filling

1 cup 1% lowfat cottage cheese

16 ounces Neufchatel cream cheese, softened

1¼ cups brown sugar

1 Tbsp. water

2 tsp. vanilla

¼ cup flour

1 egg plus 1 egg white

Sauce

⅓ cup evaporated milk

2½ Tbsp. brown sugar

1 tsp. vanilla

1 Tbsp. pecans, chopped (optional)

Preheat oven to 325°.

Combine crumbs and sugar; sprinkle onto bottom of a lightly greased 8-inch springform pan, and set aside. In food processor, blend cottage cheese until smooth.

Mix in Neufchatel cheese, brown sugar, water, and vanilla. Add flour; blend until smooth, scraping twice. Add egg and egg white; mix just until incorporated. Carefully pour filling into pan. Smooth top, and bake for 45 minutes.

Turn oven off and let cheesecake remain in oven 30 minutes. Remove from oven, let cool, then chill several hours. For sauce, bring milk, brown sugar, and vanilla to a boil. Reduce heat and cook 1 to 1½ minutes, stirring constantly. Remove from heat; stir in pecans and let cool slightly.

To serve, drizzle sauce over cheesecake.

Nutritional information:
Calories per serving: 230
Fat grams per serving: 8

When ABC's "Good Morning, America" announced its "Cut-the-Calories Cook-Off" contest in 1999, a Raleigh resident took the cake in prizes. Jan Curry made this winning cheesecake on the "Good Morning, America" kitchen set in front of millions of viewers and alongside then-host Diane Sawyer and then-"GMA" food editor Sara Moulton.

Pumpkin Cheesecake | Serves 10

Our State, November 2006

Crust

1½ cups graham cracker crumbs

¼ cup sugar

¾ cup butter, melted

Filling

3 8-ounce packages cream cheese

1 cup sugar

¼ cup brown sugar, firmly packed

1 15-ounce can solid-pack pumpkin

2 eggs

⅔ cup evaporated milk

2 Tbsp. cornstarch

1¼ tsp. ground cinnamon

½ tsp. nutmeg

Topping

1 16-ounce container sour cream, room temperature

¼ cup sugar (or slightly more to taste)

1 tsp. vanilla

ground cinnamon cinnamon sticks

Crust

Combine ingredients, and put mixture in oiled 9-inch springform pan. Bake at 350° for 6 to 8 minutes. Do not brown.

Filling

Beat cream cheese with sugars until fluffy. Add pumpkin, eggs, evaporated milk, cornstarch, cinnamon, and nutmeg. Mix well. Bake at 350° for 55 to 60 minutes.

Topping

Combine first three ingredients, and mix until smooth. Spread topping over warm cheesecake, and bake at 350° for 8 minutes. Cool on wire rack. Chill for several hours or overnight. Remove pan, and garnish with ground cinnamon and cinnamon sticks.

— Plate and Palette: A Collection of Fine Art and Food from Beaufort County, *Beaufort County Arts Council, Washington, 2001.*

White Chocolate Cheesecake Tart with Cranberries

Our State, December 2008

Tart

6 ounces graham crackers, broken into large pieces

6 Tbsp. unsalted butter, melted

1 large egg white

Filling

1 pound cream cheese, softened

1 tsp. vanilla extract

Grated zest of 1 orange, about 1 tsp.

1 cup white chocolate chips

1 cup heavy cream

¾ cup powdered sugar

Topping

2 cups fresh cranberries

½ cup plus 2 Tbsp. granulated sugar

juice of 1 orange, about 6 Tbsp.

Preheat oven to 375°. In the bowl of a food processor fitted with the blade attachment, process graham crackers into crumbs. Drizzle in melted butter with the motor running; stir in egg white by hand. Transfer filling into a greased 9-inch fluted tart pan with a removable bottom that's been lined with parchment paper. Press crust into the base and up the sides of the pan.

Bake until set and golden brown, about 20 minutes. Let cool to room temperature while preparing filling.

In the bowl of an electric mixer fitted with the paddle attachment, beat cream cheese, vanilla, and orange zest together until combined and smooth. Next, melt white chocolate chips in a microwave-safe bowl in 30-second increments until melted. Beat melted chocolate into cream cheese. Transfer mixture into a separate large bowl, and clean mixing bowl. Set bowl back into place on electric mixer, and fit with the whisk attachment. Whisk together heavy cream and powdered sugar starting on low speed and increasing to medium-high speed until stiff peaks form. Fold whipped cream into cream cheese mixture. Smooth filling into cooled graham cracker tart. Let chill for about 2 hours or until set.

When ready to serve, make the topping. In a small saucepan set over medium-high heat, combine cranberries, sugar, and orange juice. Cook, stirring occasionally, until bubbly, about 8 minutes. Reduce heat to medium-low, and cook until thickened, about 3 minutes. Let cool to room temperature before topping tart.

— Charlotte Fekete, Birmingham, Alabama

Lemon Goat Cheese Cheesecake with Blackberry Sauce | Makes one 9-inch cake

Our State, May 2010

Crust

5 ounces graham crackers, crushed

6 Tbsp. unsalted butter, melted

Cake

16 ounces cream cheese, softened

12 ounces fresh goat cheese (chevre), softened

¼ cup sour cream

1½ cups sugar

grated zest of one lemon

2 tsp. vanilla extract

4 large eggs

Sauce

about 10 ounces fresh blackberries, roughly chopped

⅓ cup sugar

juice of one lemon

Preheat oven to 350°. Process crushed graham crackers in the base of a food processor fitted with the blade attachment until finely ground. Add melted butter, and pulse until mixture comes together; press into the bottom of a 9-inch springform pan. Let crust chill in the freezer while preparing the cake.

Place cream cheese, goat cheese, sour cream, and sugar in the base of an electric mixer fitted with the paddle attachment; beat until creamy. Add lemon zest and vanilla extract; beat until combined. Add eggs, one at a time, using a spatula to scrape down the sides of the bowl after each addition; beat until combined. Pour over chilled crust. Place cake on a baking sheet, and bake for about 50 to 55 minutes. (Cake should be set around the edges and wobbly in the center.) Remove cake from oven, and let cool completely. Once cool, carefully run a knife around the edge. Let chill in refrigerator for at least 8 hours.

While cake chills, make the blackberry sauce. Combine blackberries, sugar, and lemon juice in a small saucepan set over medium-high heat. Let cook until a slightly thickened sauce forms, about 10 to 12 minutes. Transfer to a small bowl, and let cool to room temperature; chill.

To cut cheesecake, run a large, sharp knife under very hot water, and carefully pat dry; cut into slices. Serve with blackberry sauce on the side.

— Charlotte Fekete, Birmingham, Alabama

Old-Fashioned Sugar Cookies | page 50

Cookies

Old-Fashioned
Sugar Cookies

Mom's Sugar Cookies

Double Chocolate
Sandwich Cookies

Easy Devil-icious Cookies

Butterscotch Pecan Cookies

Peanut Butter Promises

Carolina Snowballs

Coconut Oatmeal Cookies

Jeff's Bourbon Balls

Oatmeal Cranberry White
Chocolate Cookies

Dark Secrets

Phyllis's Ginger Cookies

Soft Ginger Cookies

Peanut Butter Delights

Christmas Cookies

Elementary Ranger Cookies

Crunchy Cookies

Coconut Dream Bars

Stained Glass Cookies

Spiced Brownies

Turtle Bars

Apple Oatmeal Cookies

Anna's Oatmeal Cookies

Cranberry Cookies

Old-Fashioned Sugar Cookies | Makes about 96 cookies

Our State, August 1995

1 cup softened butter

1 cup sugar

2 eggs, lightly beaten

1 tsp. vanilla

2½ to 3 cups all-purpose flour

½ tsp. salt

½ tsp. baking soda

Cream together butter and sugar until light and fluffy. Beat in eggs, blending well. Blend in vanilla. Sift together the flour, salt, and soda. Stir in flour, a little at a time, until a stiff dough forms. Refrigerate dough for several hours or overnight. When ready to bake, roll out a little dough at a time on a surface lightly coated with confectioners' sugar. Cut dough into shapes and place cookies on a greased baking sheet. If desired, lightly sprinkle cookies with additional granulated sugar. Bake at 350° for 12 to 15 minutes or until golden brown.

Mom's Sugar Cookies | Makes 48 cookies

Our State, October 2007

2½ cups sugar

2 eggs

1½ sticks butter, melted

½ cup honey

1 tsp. vanilla

4 cups self-rising flour

Mix sugar and eggs thoroughly. Add butter, honey, and vanilla; mix well. Mix in flour, and knead until well blended. Roll out on a floured surface, and cut into desired shapes. (Use an iced tea glass turned upside down if you don't have a cookie cutter.) Bake at 350° for about 10 minutes, or until light brown.

Emily Dorsey of Franklin County counts these cookies among her favorite desserts. The recipe was submitted to Our State *by her daughter, Jackie Parrish of Raleigh, who recommends these cookies crushed, topped with ice-cold milk, and eaten with a spoon.*

Double Chocolate Sandwich Cookies | Makes about 24 sandwich cookies

Our State, February 2010

Cookies

- 1 stick unsalted butter, softened
- 1½ cups granulated sugar
- 3 large eggs
- 2⅓ cups all-purpose flour
- ⅓ cup cocoa powder, sifted (plus extra to shape cookies)
- 1 tsp. baking powder pinch of salt

Filling

- ¾ cup heavy cream
- 8 ounces semisweet chocolate, chopped

Preheat oven to 325°. Line 4 baking sheets with parchment paper, and set aside. Place butter and sugar in the base of a stand mixer fitted with the paddle attachment, and beat until creamy. Add eggs, and beat. Add flour, cocoa powder, baking powder, and salt; mix until combined and dough comes together.

Shape the cookies. Using cocoa-powder dusted hands, roll about 2 tsp. of dough into a ball. Place ball on baking sheet and flatten slightly. Repeat until all dough is used, placing about 12 cookies on each baking sheet. Bake in batches until cookies are set, about 15 to 18 minutes. Let cool. While the cookies cool, make the filling. Heat heavy cream in a small saucepan until just simmering. Remove from heat; add chocolate. Stir until smooth and chocolate is melted; transfer to a small bowl. Chill in refrigerator about 1 hour or until filling is thickened and resembles the consistency of store-bought icing.

To finish the cookies, divide and spread filling equally onto the bottoms of half of the cookies. Top with the plain cookies to create sandwiches.

— Charlotte Fekete, Birmingham, Alabama

Easy Devil-icious Cookies | Makes 4 dozen

Our State, December 2004

- **1 box devil's food cake mix**
- **2 eggs, slightly beaten**
- **1 Tbsp. water**
- **½ cup shortening**
- **½ cup chopped pecans**

Preheat oven to 375°. Combine cake mix, eggs, water, and shortening. Mix with a spoon until well blended. Mix in pecans. Shape dough into balls the size of small walnuts. Roll balls in powdered sugar. Place on greased baking sheets. Bake at 375° for 8 to 10 minutes.

*At the Lee County Enrichment Center in Sanford, a group of bakers known as "The Cookie Cutters" — Emma Grace Jones, Mary Ruth Deese, Ruth Conder, Ruth Brewner, Betty Johnson, Sylvia Thomas, and Nancy McDowell — get together to supply the center's Bottomless Cookie Jar. The group shared with us their recipes for Easy Devil-icious Cookies and Butterscotch Pecan Cookies (***below***).*

Butterscotch Pecan Cookies | Makes 4 dozen

Our State, December 2004

- **1 box butter cake mix**
- **1 box instant butterscotch pudding mix**
- **¼ cup all purpose flour**
- **¾ cup vegetable oil**
- **1 egg**
- **1 cup chopped pecans**

In a mixing bowl, combine the first five ingredients; mix well. Stir in pecans (the dough will be crumbly). Shape teaspoonfuls of dough into individual balls and place on greased baking sheets. Bake at 350° for 10 to 12 minutes or until golden brown. (For a softer, chewy cookie, remove from the oven a little earlier.) Cool, and remove from pans.

— "The Cookie Cutters," Lee County Enrichment Center, Sanford

Peanut Butter Promises | Makes 3 dozen

Our State, February 2005

- 1¼ cups unbleached white flour
- ¼ tsp. baking powder
- ¾ tsp. baking soda
- ¼ tsp. salt
- ¼ cup butter
- ½ cup crunchy peanut butter
- ½ cup sugar
- ½ cup mild honey
- 1 egg

Sift the flour, baking powder, soda, and salt into a small bowl, and set aside. In a large bowl, beat the butter, peanut butter, sugar, honey, and egg until well blended. Add the dry ingredients, and mix thoroughly. Cover, and chill 2 hours.

Preheat the oven to 375°. Grease baking sheets lightly. Roll bits of dough into walnut-sized balls, and place 2 inches apart on baking sheets. Flatten with a fork to make a crisscross pattern. Bake 10 to 12 minutes. Allow cookies to rest on the pan a minute before transferring to a rack to cool.

— Erica Derr, Greensboro

Carolina Snowballs | Makes 36 snowballs

Our State, February 2004

- 8 ounces mixed dried fruits (apricots, cherries, pineapple, for example)
- 2½ cups unsweetened coconut flakes, toasted (available at health food stores, or if unavailable, just rinse the sweetened coconut under cold water, and pat dry before toasting)
- ¾ cup coarsely chopped walnuts
- ¾ cup sweetened condensed milk
- ¾ cup confectioners' sugar

Chop dried fruit into ¼-inch pieces. In a medium bowl, mix together fruit, coconut, nuts, and sweetened condensed milk. Sift confectioners' sugar onto a large plate. Firmly form ¾-inch balls of the mixture, and roll them through the sugar to coat completely.

— Erica Derr, Greensboro

Coconut Oatmeal Cookies | Makes 36 cookies

Our State, February 2005

1¼ cup flour

1 tsp. baking powder

1 tsp. baking soda

½ tsp. salt

½ cup white sugar

½ cup firmly packed brown sugar

½ cup butter, softened

1 egg

½ tsp. vanilla

1 cup uncooked regular oats

1 cup coconut

Combine flour, baking powder, baking soda, and salt in a large mixing bowl. Add sugars, butter, egg, and vanilla. Beat until smooth (about 2 minutes). Stir in oats and coconut. Shape dough into 1-inch balls. Place on greased cookie sheets, and bake at 350° for 8 to 10 minutes or until lightly browned.

Our State *readers remember a down-home eatery, Fran's Front Porch, as having some of the best homemade desserts in North Carolina. Although the restaurant is now closed, we are happy to have acquired the cookie recipe from* The Best in Southern Cooking from Fran's Front Porch, *Liberty, N.C. 1980. Out of print.*

Jeff's Bourbon Balls | Makes 40 balls

Our State, December 2005

6-ounce package chocolate bits

½ cup granulated sugar

3 Tbsp. light corn syrup

½ cup bourbon

1½ cups vanilla wafers, finely crushed

1 cup walnuts or pecans, finely chopped

powdered sugar, sifted

Melt chocolate in top of double boiler. Remove from heat. Stir in sugar and corn syrup. Add bourbon, and blend well. Combine vanilla wafer crumbs and nuts in a large bowl. Add chocolate mixture, and blend well. Form into 1-inch balls. Roll in powdered sugar. Place in airtight container for 3 to 10 days.

— Modern Recipes from Historic Wilmington, *Lower Cape Fear Historical Society, Wilmington, 2003.*

Oatmeal Cranberry White Chocolate Cookies | Makes about 60 cookies

Our State, December 2005

1 cup butter, softened

1 cup light brown sugar

2 eggs

2 cups oats

2 cups flour

½ tsp. salt

½ tsp. baking soda

1½ cups dried cranberries

1 cup white chocolate chunks or chips

Preheat oven to 375°. Beat butter and brown sugar until light and creamy. Add eggs, one at a time, beating well after each addition. Combine oats, flour, salt, and baking soda in a separate mixing bowl. Add wet mixture to dry mixture in several stages, mixing well after each addition. Stir in dried cranberries and white chocolate chips, mixing just to combine. Drop by rounded teaspoonfuls onto an ungreased cookie sheet. Bake 10 to 12 minutes or until golden brown.

— The Fresh Market and Friends, *The Fresh Market Inc., Greensboro, 2003.*

Dark Secrets | Makes 12-16 small bars

Our State, February 2005

1 cup sugar

2 Tbsp. butter, melted

3 eggs, unbeaten

1 cup pecans, chopped

1 cup dates, chopped

1 can (3.5 ounce) coconut

5 Tbsp. flour

1 tsp. baking powder

1 package (6 ounce)

chocolate chips

Combine all ingredients. Spread in a 9-x-9-inch pan, and bake at 350° for approximately 20 minutes. If an 8-x-8-inch pan is used, baked for 30 minutes.

— Out of Our League, *Junior League of Greensboro, 1978.*

Phyllis's Ginger Cookies | Makes 48 cookies

Our State, October 2007

¼ cup plus 2 Tbsp. vegetable shortening

½ stick plus 2 Tbsp. butter, softened

1 cup sugar

1 egg, beaten

¼ cup molasses

2 cups unsifted all-purpose flour

1 tsp. baking soda

½ tsp. salt

1 tsp. cinnamon

1 tsp. ground cloves

1 tsp. ground ginger

Preheat oven to 350°. Cream together shortening, butter, sugar, egg, and molasses. Stir in flour, baking soda, salt, cinnamon, cloves, and ginger. Roll dough into 1-inch balls. Bake on an ungreased cookie sheet for 12 to 15 minutes (cookies should be crinkly and soft on top when done).

— North Carolina Bed and Breakfast Cookbook, *3D Press, Boulder, CO. 2005.*

Soft Ginger Cookies | Makes 24-36 cookies

Our State, December 2006

2½ cups flour

2 tsp. ground ginger

1 tsp. baking soda

¾ tsp. ground cinnamon

½ tsp. ground cloves

¼ tsp. salt (optional)

¾ cup margarine or butter, room temperature

2 cups sugar, divided

1 egg

¼ cup molasses

Preheat oven to 350°. Sift together flour, soda, spices, and salt, and set aside. Beat margarine until fluffy. Add 1 cup sugar gradually and beat until blended. Add egg and molasses. Stir in flour mixture, and blend well. Roll rounded tablespoonfuls of dough into balls about 1½ inches in diameter. Roll each ball in sugar, and place 8 balls on each ungreased baking sheet. Bake 10 minutes or until lightly browned and puffy. Do not overbake. Transfer to wire rack to cool.

— With Heart and Hand, *Women's Fellowship of Home Moravian Church, Winston-Salem; Lynne R. Holton contributed this recipe to the cookbook*

Peanut Butter Delights | Makes about 30 cookies

Our State, October 2007

2 cups sugar

½ cup evaporated milk

⅓ cup cocoa

½ cup butter

3 cups quick-cooking oatmeal

¾ cup peanut butter

Place sugar, milk, cocoa, and butter into a heavy saucepan, and bring to a boil, stirring occasionally. Let the mixture boil hard for about 1½ minutes. Add the peanut butter, and then stir in the oatmeal. When combined, drop by teaspoonfuls onto waxed paper. Let cool.

— Betty Hamilton, Star

Christmas Cookies | Makes about 100 medium-size cookies

Our State, December 2005

1 cup soft shortening

1 cup white sugar

1 cup brown sugar

2 eggs, unbeaten

1 tsp. vanilla extract

2 cups flour

1 tsp. baking soda

½ tsp. baking powder

½ tsp. salt

2 cups quick oatmeal

2 cups corn flakes, crushed

1 cup pecans, chopped

1 cup raisins

1 cup flaked coconut

1 cup red candied cherries

1 cup green candied cherries

Preheat oven to 375°. Cream shortening and sugars. Add eggs and vanilla extract. Sift in dry ingredients. Add oatmeal, corn flakes, raisins, pecans, coconut, and candied cherries. Work with hands until well mixed. Form into small balls, and press slightly on cookie sheet. Bake 8 to 10 minutes.

— River Rations: Recipes and Recollections of Rural Living*, Whitline Ink, Boonville, 1998.*

Elementary Ranger Cookies | Makes 72 cookies

Our State, October 2007

1 cup butter, softened to room temperature

1 cup sugar

1 cup brown sugar, packed

2 eggs, beaten

2 cups all-purpose flour, sifted

½ tsp. baking powder

½ tsp. salt

½ tsp. baking soda

1 tsp. vanilla extract

2 cups rolled oats

2 cups cornflakes, lightly crushed

½ cup flaked coconut (optional)

½ cup chocolate chips

½ cup chopped walnuts

Cream butter with sugars until light and fluffy. Beat in eggs, one at a time. Add baking powder, salt, and baking soda to sifted flour. Stir flour mixture into butter mixture. Add remaining ingredients, and stir until blended. Drop by rounded teaspoonfuls onto an ungreased baking sheet. Bake at 375° for 8 to 10 minutes.

Erica Derr, who wrote Our State*'s "Carolina Kitchen" column from 2003-2007, remembers these cookies from her sixth-grade after-school baking sessions.*

Crunchy Cookies | Makes 72 cookies

Our State, March 1997

1 cup sugar

1 cup brown sugar, packed

1 cup butter, softened

1 cup cooking oil

1 egg, lightly beaten

2 tsp. vanilla

3½ cups all-purpose flour

1 scant tsp. salt

1 tsp. baking soda

1 tsp. cream of tartar

1 cup flaked coconut

1 cup crisp rice cereal

1 cup uncooked oatmeal

½ cup chopped pecans

Cream sugars with butter and oil. Beat in egg and vanilla. Sift together the flour, salt, soda, and cream of tartar. Add gradually to creamed mixture. Stir in coconut, both cereals, and nuts. Drop mixture by scant tablespoonfuls onto a cookie sheet. Flatten each cookie slightly. Bake at 350° for 12 to 15 minutes.

Edie Low of Rock Hill, South Carolina, wrote Our State*'s "Tar Heel Recipes" column throughout the 1980s, '90s, and 2000s.*

Coconut Dream Bars | Makes 8-10 servings

Our State, February 2008

Crust

½ cup butter

½ cup light brown sugar

pinch of salt

1 cup flour, sifted

Topping

2 eggs

1 cup light brown sugar

3 Tbsp. flour, sifted

pinch of salt

1½ cups fresh grated coconut

1 cup chopped walnuts

1 tsp. vanilla extract

Crust

Cream butter, sugar, and salt together until fluffy. Add flour. Pack into a greased 8-inch round cake pan, and bake in 350° oven for 10 minutes. Remove from oven, and top with filling.

Topping

Beat eggs and other ingredients together. Spread on top of crust mixture. Return to oven, and bake until browned and firm, about 15 to 20 minutes. Cool before cutting.

— Sweet Tooth: Down Home Meals and Blue Ribbon Desserts *by Sarah Ann Spaugh, Carolina Avenue Press, Boonville, N.C. 2004.*

Stained Glass Cookies

Our State, December 2000

½ cup margarine

½ cup sugar

½ cup honey

1 egg, beaten

1 tsp. vanilla extract

3 cups flour

1 tsp. baking powder

½ tsp. baking soda

½ tsp. salt

9 ounces LifeSaver candies, approximately

Preheat oven to 350°. Cream margarine, sugar, honey, egg, and vanilla in a bowl. Mix in flour, baking powder, baking soda, and salt. Cover tightly, and refrigerate for 2 hours. Turn dough onto a lightly floured surface, and roll out to 1/4 inch thickness. With a set of nesting cookie cutters, first use the largest size cutter to make the cookies, then use the smallest of that shape in the center of the cookies to make the "windows." Place the cut-out shapes on baking sheets lined with foil. Repeat with remaining dough. Crush each color of candies separately between layers of wax paper. Spoon the crushed candy into "windows" of cookies. Bake for 6 to 8 minutes, or until candy is melted and cookies are lightly brown. Cool completely before removing from foil. *— Erica Derr, Greensboro*

Spiced Brownies

Our State, February 2010

- 1 stick unsalted butter, diced
- 6 ounces semisweet chocolate, broken into pieces
- 1 Tbsp. instant coffee granules
- 1½ cups granulated sugar
- 3 large eggs
- 1 tsp. vanilla extract
- pinch of salt
- 1 cup all-purpose flour
- ¼ tsp. ground cinnamon
- ⅛ tsp. cayenne pepper, or to taste

Preheat oven to 375°. Spray an 8-x-8-inch baking pan with nonstick spray and set aside. Melt butter and chocolate together in a saucepan set over low heat. Stir in instant coffee. Add sugar, and stir to combine. Remove from heat, and let cool slightly. In a large bowl, whisk together eggs, vanilla, and salt. Slowly whisk in chocolate mixture. Stir in flour, cinnamon, and cayenne. Pour batter into prepared pan, and bake for about 40 minutes or until set. (Brownies are done when a toothpick inserted in the center comes out with a light crumb and a little unbaked batter.) Let cool completely, cut into squares, and serve.

Food stylist and recipe writer Charlotte Fekete began writing Our State*'s "Carolina Kitchen" column in 2008.*

Turtle Bars | Makes about 48 1-x-2 inch bars

The State, November 1994

- ½ cup vegetable shortening
- ¼ cup butter
- 1¼ cups brown sugar, packed
- 2 Tbsp. milk
- 1 tsp. vanilla
- 1 egg, lightly beaten
- 1¾ cups all-purpose flour
- ½ tsp. salt
- ¾ tsp. baking soda
- 1½ cups semisweet chocolate bits
- 1 package (14 ounces) caramels
- 1 Tbsp. water

Blend shortening, butter, and sugar until creamy. Blend in milk and vanilla. Beat in egg. Sift together the flour, salt, and baking soda. Stir into creamed mixture only until blended. Stir in chocolate. Spread two-thirds of dough evenly in a buttered 9-x-13-x-2-inch pan. Combine caramels and water in top of a double boiler, but not touching bubbling water. Stir constantly until caramels melt. Spread melted caramel on top of dough in pan, to within a half-inch of edge. Spread remaining third of dough in dollops over top of caramel layer. Bake at 350° for 25 to 30 minutes, or until golden brown. Be careful not to overbake. Cool completely on a rack. Cut into bars.

Candy and cookies are naturals whenever a sweet tooth cries for nourishment. Maggie Peeler of Mountain Grove sent this recipe for readers to try. It's actually a cookie, rather than the candy also called a turtle.

Apple-Oatmeal Cookies | Makes approx. 36 cookies

Our State, December 1994

- ½ cup butter or margarine
- ¼ cup solid vegetable shortening
- 1½ cups brown sugar, packed
- 1 egg
- ⅓ cup apple juice
- 2 Tbsp. honey
- 1½ tsp. vanilla
- 3 cups uncooked, unflavored quick oats
- 1 cup all-purpose flour
- ½ tsp. baking soda
- ½ tsp. salt
- ¼ tsp. ground cinnamon
- 1 cup raisins
- 1 cup chopped nuts
- 1 large tart apple (peeled, cored, chopped)

Beat butter, shortening, and sugar together until soft and blended. Beat in egg, juice, honey, and vanilla. Place oats in a large bowl. Sift together the flour, soda, salt, and cinnamon. Stir into oats. Blend oat-flour mixture into butter mixture. Dough will be stiff. Stir in nuts and apple just until blended. Drop by heaping teaspoonfuls onto a greased cookie sheet. Dough should be 2 to 3 inches apart to allow for spreading as cookies bake. Bake at 375° for 8 to 10 minutes, or until light brown. Cool 2 minutes on baking sheet, then remove to a rack to cool completely.

— Fanny Shephard, Asheville

Anna's Oatmeal Cookies | Makes about 24 cookies

Our State, February 1993

- **1¼ cups butter flavored shortening, divided**
- **1½ cups lightly packed light brown sugar**
- **¾ cup granulated sugar**
- **4 egg whites**
- **1½ cups all-purpose flour**
- **1½ tsp. baking soda**
- **1½ tsp. salt**
- **3 cups quick rolled oats, uncooked**
- **4 tsp. vanilla, divided**
- **2 cups confectioners' sugar**
- **Milk**

Combine 1 cup shortening with the brown and granulated sugars. Beat at medium speed of mixer until well blended. Beat in egg whites. Sift together the flour, soda, and salt. Add to creamed mixture at low speed, blending well. Stir in oats and one tablespoon vanilla; mix well. Drop by rounded tablespoonfuls two inches apart onto an ungreased baking sheet. Bake at 350° for 8 minutes or until lightly brown. Cool 30 seconds before removing to a rack to cool. Meanwhile, combine confectioners' sugar with the remaining quarter-cup of shortening and one teaspoon of vanilla. Beat at low speed with enough milk to make spreading consistency. Spread on bottom of half of the cookies. Top with remaining cookies.

Beth Layton of Lewisville and her daughter, Anna, took the state champion prize in the American Baking Celebration, co-sponsored by Good Housekeeping *magazine and Crisco, in 1993.*

Cranberry Cookies | Makes 2-3 dozen cookies

Our State, December 1993

½ cup butter

¼ cup solid shortening

1¼ cups brown sugar, packed

1 egg

⅓ cup milk

1½ tsp. vanilla

1 tsp. grated orange peel

1 cup all-purpose flour

½ tsp. baking soda

½ tsp. salt

3 cups uncooked quick oats

1 cup dried cranberries

1 cup coarsely chopped nuts

Beat butter, shortening, and sugar together until light and fluffy. Stir in egg, milk, vanilla, and orange peel, then beat at medium speed of mixer until well blended. Sift flour with baking soda and salt, then blend with oats. Add to creamed mixture, stirring just until blended. Mixture will be stiff. Stir in cranberries and nuts. Place a tablespoon of dough at a time on a greased cookie sheet, each two inches apart. Bake at 375° until golden, about 10 minutes. Cool a minute or so on cookie sheet, then remove to a rack to finish cooling.

— Susan Masson, Asheville

Peach Ice Cream #1 | page 68

Ice Cream

Peach Ice Cream #1

Our State, July 1999

10-12 ripe peaches, peeled and sliced

1 small package vanilla instant pudding

1 can sweetened condensed milk

¾ cup sugar

1 tsp. vanilla flavoring

Milk (about ½ gallon)

In large bowl, chop peaches into small bits. Add vanilla pudding, sweetened condensed milk, sugar, and vanilla flavoring. Stir well. Pour into ice cream freezer. Add milk to fill to full line.

— Rhonda Chappell, Candor
1997 North Carolina Peach Festival Cooking Contest Winner

Peach Ice Cream #2

Our State, August 2002

8-10 ripe peaches

1 cup sugar

½ package instant vanilla pudding

1 can sweetened condensed milk

1 pint heavy cream

1½ quarts whole milk

6 eggs

Dip each peach in boiling water to remove skins. Slice and toss with sugar in a medium bowl. Set aside. Mix together pudding, condensed milk, cream, and whole milk in a heavy-bottomed saucepan. Beat the eggs in a separate bowl, and add to the milk mixture. Cook slowly until the mixture barely coats the back of a wooden spoon. Remove from heat, and stir in the peaches. Freeze in ice cream maker according to the manufacturer's instructions.

— Sugar Pie & Jelly Roll *by Robbin Gourley, Algonquin Books of Chapel Hill, 2000.*

Icy Chocolate Milkshake | Makes 2 servings

Our State, July 1999

2 cups low-fat chocolate milk, divided

Pour ½ cup of milk into ice-cube tray and freeze into cubes. When ready to serve, pour remaining 1½ cups milk into a blender. Add frozen milk cubes. Process until slushy. Serve at once.

Old-Fashioned Homemade Ice Cream | Makes 16 servings

Our State, July 2004

- 2 Tbsp. cornstarch
- 2 quarts milk
- 6 egg yolks, beaten
- 3½ cups sugar
- 1 quart half-and-half
- 6 egg whites, stiffly beaten
- 2 Tbsp. vanilla extract
- 1 cup whipping cream

Combine the cornstarch with ½ cup of the milk in a 3-quart saucepan; mix well. Stir in the egg yolks, sugar, half-and-half, and enough of the remaining milk to fill the saucepan. Cook over medium heat for 20 minutes, stirring frequently. Let stand until cool. Strain into a bowl. Fold in the egg whites. Stir in the vanilla and whipping cream. Pour into a freezer container. Pour in the remaining milk to the fill line. Freeze using ice cream maker manufacturer's directions.

— A Taste of North Carolina: A Collection of Recipes from Festivals and Events in North Carolina. *Bluewater Marketing, Wilmington, N.C. 1996.*

Blueberry Honey Ice Cream | Makes 1 quart

Our State, August 1997

- 6 large egg yolks
- 1 cup heavy cream
- ¾ cup blueberry honey or other flavorful, good quality honey
- a pinch of salt
- 2 tsp. pure vanilla extract
- 2 cups whole milk

In the top of a double boiler, whisk together egg yolks, cream, honey, and salt until golden yellow in color. Place mixture over boiling water in the double boiler. Stir with a wooden spoon until mixture reaches between 165° and 175°. Use candy thermometer to test the temperature. Continue to stir, holding mixture at this temperature for 5 to 10 minutes, until it coats the back of the spoon. When the custard is done, remove from heat and add vanilla and milk, whisking to blend thoroughly. Strain through a fine-mesh sieve and chill completely, preferably overnight. Transfer to an ice cream maker and freeze following manufacturer's instructions.

In 1997, Nancy Quaintance of Greensboro wrote Our State*'s "Tar Heel Living" column.*

Cheerwine Ice Cream | Makes about 5 cups

Our State, March 2010

- 2 large eggs
- 1 cup granulated sugar
- 1 cup heavy cream
- ½ cup plus 2 Tbsp. sweetened condensed milk (about half a 14-ounce can)
- ¾ cup evaporated milk (about half a 12-ounce can)
- 1¼ cups Cheerwine, chilled
- 1 cup whole milk

In a large heat-proof bowl, whisk together eggs and sugar until pale yellow and combined; set aside.

In a small saucepan set over medium heat, bring heavy cream just to a boil. Very slowly, add hot cream to egg mixture, whisking constantly. Set bowl over a saucepan of simmering water, making sure the bottom of the bowl does not touch the water. Cook, stirring occasionally, until the mixture coats the back of a spoon, about 4 minutes.

Remove from heat and add condensed and evaporated milks. Chill in refrigerator until completely cold. Whisk in Cheerwine and milk. Freeze in ice cream maker according to manufacturer's instructions until the mixture has the consistency of soft serve. Place ice cream in freezer until set to your liking.

— Charlotte Fekete, Birmingham, Alabama

Peach and Strawberry Sorbet | Makes 1 quart

Our State, August 2008

- 3 pounds peaches, peeled and quartered
- 1 pound strawberries, halved
- 1 cup granulated sugar

Puree peaches and strawberries in the work bowl of a food processor fitted with the blade attachment until smooth. Strain puree, and discard remaining pulp. In a saucepan on medium heat, combine 1 cup strained puree with sugar. Cook for about 3 minutes or until sugar is completely dissolved. Stir sweetened puree back into remaining puree, and refrigerate until chilled. Freeze mixture in an ice cream maker according to manufacturer's instructions, and transfer to freezer to set.

— Charlotte Fekete, Birmingham, Alabama

Choco-Nana Pops | Makes 6 servings

Our State, July 1999

- 1 cup low-fat chocolate milk
- 1 ripe banana, peeled
- 2 Tbsp. chocolate syrup
- 1 tsp. vanilla
- 6 (3 oz.) paper cups
- Aluminum foil
- 5 popsicle sticks

Pour milk into blender; cut banana into pieces and add to milk. Add chocolate syrup and vanilla. Blend on high speed until thick, about 1 minute. Divide mixture among the cups. Cover each cup with foil. Poke popsicle sticks through foil and into mixture.
Freeze until firm. A quick dip in hot water lets you easily remove the cup from the popsicle, and the foil prevents dripping.

— National Dairy Association

Blueberry Lemonade Popsicles | Makes 4-6 servings

Our State, June 2005

Lemonade:

- 1 cup sugar
- 6 cups water
- finely grated zest of 1 lemon
- 1 pint fresh blueberries, rinsed, stems removed
- juice of 6 large lemons
- ice
- slices of fresh lemon, for garnish

Mix sugar, water, and lemon zest in a saucepan. Warm over medium-high heat, stirring to dissolve the sugar. Once sugar has completely dissolved, remove pan from heat, and pour mixture into a large glass pitcher. Combine blueberries with the lemon juice in a blender, and puree. Add to the pitcher, and stir well to blend. Pour lemonade through a sieve to remove the blueberry skins.
Chill from 2 hours up to 24 hours. Pour lemonade over tall, ice-filled glasses, and garnish each with a lemon slice.

Blueberry Lemonade Popsicles
Make the above recipe; add a half pint of whole blueberries, rinsed and stems removed. Pour into popsicle molds, and freeze.

— Erica Derr, Greensboro

Mama Dip's Pecan Pie | page 74

Pies, Cobblers, and Sonkers

Mama Dip's Pecan Pie
Sweet Potato Pie
Pecan Pie
Strawberry Rhubarb Pie
Easy Freezy Lemon Pie
Sugar Cream Pie
Pear Pie
Neighbors' Apple Pie
Minnie's Harvest Apple Pie
Double-Coconut Pie
100-year-old Chess Pie
Harvest Watermelon Pie
Old-Fashioned Egg Custard Pie
Jarrett House Vinegar Pie
Our Favorite Fresh Strawberry Pie
Strawberry Pie
Apple Cobbler
Peach Blueberry Cobbler
Blueberry Buckle
Bob Garner's Peach Cobbler
Rustic Peach Tarts
Lemony Peach and Blueberry Crisp
Insanely Easy Blackberry Cobbler
No-Bake Blueberry Sonker
Maxine Dockery's Sweet Potato Sonker
Individual Pecan and Chocolate Tarts
Blueberry Tart

Mama Dip's Pecan Pie | Makes 8 servings

Our State, November 1999

- 1 stick butter or margarine
- 1 cup sugar
- 1 cup light Karo syrup
- 3 eggs, beaten
- 1 cup chopped pecans
- 1 unbaked 9-inch pie shell

Preheat oven to 350°. In a saucepan, melt the butter, but don't let it brown. Mix in the sugar and Karo syrup and cook, stirring, over medium heat until the sugar dissolves. Stir in the eggs. Mix well. Stir in the pecans. Pour into the pie shell and bake for 1 hour or until firm when shaken. Serves 8.

This is the pie that Mildred "Mama Dip" Council made on "Good Morning, America." For a taste of the real thing, visit Mama Dip's Kitchen at 408 West Rosemary Street in Chapel Hill; the pecan pie is nearly always on the menu.

Sweet Potato Pie | Makes 2 standard 9-inch pies

Our State, January 2010

- 3 medium sweet potatoes, about 1¾ pounds
- 6 Tbsp. unsalted butter, melted
- 1¼ cups light brown sugar
- ¾ cup half-and-half
- 3 large eggs, lightly beaten
- 1 Tbsp. all-purpose flour
- ½ tsp. ground cinnamon
- ¼ tsp. ground nutmeg
- 2 (9-inch) prepared, unbaked pie shells

Preheat oven to 350°. Prick potatoes with a fork and roast on a baking sheet until tender, about 1 hour and 15 minutes. When potatoes are cool enough to handle, scoop out flesh into a large bowl (discard peels) and mash with melted butter and brown sugar. Stir in half-and-half, eggs, flour, cinnamon, and nutmeg. Transfer mixture to the base of a food processor fitted with the blade attachment, and process until smooth. Divide filling equally between pie shells and bake for about 45 to 50 minutes, or until filling is set. Let cool, and serve with whipped cream, if desired.

— Charlotte Fekete, Birmingham, Alabama

Pecan Pie

Our State, January 2010

Crust

1½ cups all-purpose flour

1 Tbsp. granulated sugar

pinch of salt

9 Tbsp. cold unsalted butter, diced

6 Tbsp. cold water

½ tsp. apple cider vinegar

Filling

3 large eggs

2 Tbsp. unsalted butter, melted and cooled

1 cup granulated sugar

1 Tbsp. all-purpose flour

¾ cup dark corn syrup

1 tsp. vanilla extract

1½ cups chopped pecans

½ cup pecan halves

First, make the crust. Blend together flour, sugar, and salt in the work bowl of a food processor fitted with the blade attachment. Add diced butter, and pulse 20 times or until a coarse meal forms. Add water and vinegar, and process until dough is moist and in clumps. (If dough is too dry, add an extra tablespoon of water.) Turn dough out onto a floured work surface and form into a ball. Flatten into a disc and wrap in plastic wrap. Chill in refrigerator at least 2 hours.

Preheat oven to 350°. Make the filling. In a large bowl, whisk together eggs, melted butter, sugar, flour, corn syrup, and vanilla until well blended. Stir in chopped pecans and pecan halves. On a floured board, roll out chilled pie dough into a 13-inch round. Fit and trim into a 9-inch pie plate. Pour in pecan mixture. Bake until filling is set, about 1 hour and 15 minutes. Let cool before serving.

— Charlotte Fekete, Birmingham, Alabama

Strawberry Rhubarb Pie

Our State, April 1996

1 pint strawberries

1 pound rhubarb

1¾ cups sugar

⅓ cup flour, unsifted

Dash of salt

Pastry for two-crust pie

3 Tbsp. butter

Remove stems, and cut strawberries into halves. Trim rhubarb; cut into half-inch pieces. Blend together the sugar, flour, and salt. Combine strawberries and rhubarb in a bowl. Stir in sugar mixture. Line a pie pan with pastry. Pile berry mixture into a pan. Dot with butter. Place top pastry over berry mixture. Seal edges of pie. Cut slits into crust to allow steam to escape. Place foil in oven under pan to catch drips. Brush pie crust with milk, and sprinkle lightly with sugar for a crisp crust. Bake at 425° for 40 to 50 minutes. Cool 10 minutes before cutting pie.

— Charlotte Fekete, Birmingham, Alabama

Easy Freezy Lemon Pie | Makes 1 9-inch pie

Our State, March 2007

1 6-ounce package semisweet chocolate chips

3 Tbsp. butter or margarine

2 cups crisp rice cereal

¾ cup flaked coconut, toasted

2 cups lemon pie filling

1 pint vanilla ice cream frozen

whipped topping

chocolate curls

Melt chocolate chips and butter in a heavy saucepan. Add cereal and toasted coconut, and mix well. Press into buttered 9-inch pie plate; chill until firm. Pour lemon pie filling into an ice cube tray; freeze several hours until icy. Turn frozen lemon pie filling into a bowl, and beat with mixer. Cut ice cream into eighths, and add to pie filling; beat to mix. Pour into chilled cereal crust. Cover and freeze overnight. To serve, top with whipped topping and chocolate curls.

Home economist Betty Feezor earned a loyal following thanks to the recipes she made while playing host to her namesake television show on Charlotte's WBTV. This one comes from Betty Feezor's Carolina Recipes, Volume II, *WBTV, Charlotte, 1974. Out of print.*

Sugar Cream Pie

Our State, April 2005

⅔ cup sugar

½ tsp. salt

2½ Tbsp. cornstarch

1 Tbsp. flour

3 cups whole milk

3 egg yolks, slightly beaten

1 Tbsp. butter

1½ tsp. vanilla extract

1 9-inch pie crust, baked and cooled

whipped cream topping (optional)

Mix sugar, salt, cornstarch, and flour in a saucepan. Gradually stir in the milk. Cook over moderate heat, stirring constantly, until mixture thickens and boils. Boil for 1 minute, then remove from heat. Stir a little of the mixture into egg yolks. Next, blend egg yolk mixture into hot mixture in saucepan. Boil 1 minute more, stirring constantly. Remove from heat. Blend in butter and vanilla extract. Cool, stirring occasionally.

Pour into baked pie shell. Chill for 2 hours. Top with whipped topping if desired.

Variations:

Blackberry Cream Pie

Use the Sugar Cream Pie recipe above, but fold in 1 cup of thawed and drained frozen blackberries or 1 cup of washed and patted-dry fresh blackberries after cream pie mixture has cooled and before pouring into pie shell. Garnish top with berries.

Chocolate Cream Pie

Use the Sugar Cream Pie recipe, but use 1½ cups sugar, and add ½ cup semisweet chocolate chips, melted in a double boiler, after adding the butter and vanilla and before cooling.

Banana Rum Cream Pie

Use the Sugar Cream Pie recipe, but slice two or three large bananas and place in the bottom of pie shell before adding cream pie mixture or chocolate cream pie mixture. Add 1 tablespoon of dark rum to cream pie mixture after adding butter and vanilla.

— Erica Derr, Greensboro

Pear Pie

Our State, June 1996

Pastry for two-crust pie

6 pears, peeled, sliced

½ cup brown sugar, packed

¼ cup granulated sugar

Pinch of salt

½ tsp. ground ginger

¼ tsp. ground cinnamon

2 tsp. cornstarch

1 Tbsp. lemon juice

2 Tbsp. orange juice

1 Tbsp. unsalted butter

1 egg, slightly beaten

1 Tbsp. heavy cream

Place bottom crust in pie pan. Arrange pear slices evenly in crust. Combine the two sugars, salt, ginger, cinnamon, and cornstarch, blending well. Sprinkle mixture evenly over pears. Sprinkle lemon and orange juices over fruit. Cut butter into small pieces and dot pears with pieces. Place top crust on pie, seal edges, and cut slits in top so steam can escape. Beat egg with cream. Brush mixture over top crust for glaze. Bake at 400° for one hour or until golden brown and fruit is tender.

— Rachel Welborne, Jacksonville

Neighbors' Apple Pie | Makes one 7- to 8-inch pie

Our State, October 2005

- 1½ cups sifted flour
- 1 tsp. salt
- ½ cup vegetable shortening
- 2 to 3 Tbsp. ice water
- 8 cups peeled and cored apples (about 7 to 9), sliced ¼-inch thin (my neighbors like to use Pink Lady apples)
- 1 cup sugar
- 2 Tbsp. cornstarch
- 2 tsp. vanilla
- ¼ tsp. cinnamon
- 2 Tbsp. unsalted butter
- 1 Tbsp. milk
- ½ tsp. sugar plus ¼ tsp. cinnamon, mixed

Preheat oven to 425°.

Prepare piecrusts. Sift flour and salt into a large bowl. Using a pastry blender, cut shortening into flour until mixture is the consistency of small peas. Add ice water by tablespoons, sprinkling in a little at a time. Toss lightly to blend; do not mash. Add just enough water to achieve a firm dough (you might not use all the water). Divide mixture into two pieces. Place each onto a piece of wax paper, and push and press the dough together. Wrap in wax paper, and let rest 15 to 20 minutes. Meanwhile, prepare the filling. Combine apples, 1 cup sugar, cornstarch, vanilla, and ¼ tsp. cinnamon.

Roll out one ball of dough on a lightly floured surface or on a cloth-covered pastry board with a cloth-covered rolling pin. Roll out to fit a 7- to 8-inch pie pan. Transfer to pie pan. Pour filling into pie shell. Dot with butter. Roll out second ball of dough. Place on top of pie, and crimp edges to seal rim. Cut eight small vents in top crust by slashing with a sharp knife. Brush with milk. Combine ½ tsp. sugar and ¼ tsp. cinnamon, and sprinkle on top. Bake pie for 15 minutes at 425°, then reduce heat to 350°, and bake 30 minutes or until crust is golden brown.

Raleigh resident Debbie Moose, author of Deviled Eggs, Fan Fare, *and* Wings, *told* Our State *that her neighbors, Kathy and Kay, are real apple-pie people. In sharing baking tips, Kathy and Kay helped cure Moose from treating the dough like she was swatting flies.*

Minnie's Harvest Apple Pie

Our State, April 2006

3 large Granny Smith apples, peeled, cored, and sliced

1 orange, zested

1 cup fresh cranberries

⅓ cup raisins

¼ cup walnuts, chopped

¼ cup all-purpose flour

½ cup brown sugar

1 tsp. ground cinnamon

¼ tsp. ground nutmeg pie crust dough, enough for top and bottom (from your own favorite recipe)

¼ cup half-and-half

sugar, for sprinkling

Preheat the oven to 400°.

In a large bowl, combine the sliced apples, orange zest, cranberries, raisins, walnuts, flour, brown sugar, cinnamon, and nutmeg; mix well. Roll out the bottom dough, and place it into a 9-inch pan, leaving 1 inch of pie dough hanging over. Pour the pie filling into the crust. Roll out the top dough, and cut it with a scalloped pastry wheel into 15 strips. Gently twist the strips 2 or 3 times, beginning with the longest ones, and place them on top of the pie, working outward and in various angles. Gently fold the bottom crust up over the edge of the pie, and flute the edges with your fingertips. With a pastry brush, gently brush the half-and-half over the entire top crust and edges, and then sprinkle generously with sugar.

Bake until apples are cooked, about 45 to 50 minutes. (You can check the apples with a fork to make sure they are tender). Remove to a rack to cool. Serve warm or at room temperature.

Minnie Smith, a k a "The Pie Lady," owns Picnics Restaurant and Bake Shop (371 Merrimon Avenue in Asheville) and specializes in fresh-baked pies. You can try her recipe for harvest apple, or, if you don't want to bake, swing by the shop and pick one up on your way to the Parkway.

Double-Coconut Pie | Makes 6-8 servings

Our State, February 2008

Crust

7 ounces shredded sweetened coconut

3 egg whites

¼ cup flour

⅛ tsp. salt

⅛ tsp. grated nutmeg

Filling

1½ cups whole milk

3 egg yolks (save whites for meringue)

½ cup sugar

2½ Tbsp. cornstarch

1 Tbsp. butter

¾ cup shredded sweetened coconut

1 tsp. vanilla extract

¼ tsp. salt

Meringue

3 egg whites

½ cup plus 2 Tbsp. sugar

¼ cup water

1 tsp. vanilla extract

Note: This pie can also be topped with whipped cream instead of meringue.

Crust

Preheat oven to 325°. In a large bowl, mix together coconut, egg whites, flour, salt, and nutmeg. Press mixture into a greased 9-inch pie pan. Transfer to oven, and bake for 25-30 minutes or until crust is lightly browned at the edges and dry. Let cool while preparing filling.

Filling

First, scald the milk. In a small saucepan, heat milk on medium high, stirring occasionally, until milk is about to boil and small bubbles form around the rim of the pan. Remove from heat; skim off any skin that may have formed. In a separate saucepan, beat egg yolks with sugar and cornstarch until well combined. Slowly whisk in scalded milk. Transfer to medium-high heat, and cook, stirring constantly, until thickened. Remove from heat, and add butter, coconut, vanilla, and salt; stir until smooth. Chill while preparing meringue.

Meringue

In the bowl of stand mixer with whisk attachment, whisk egg whites until frothy, and slowly add 2 tablespoons sugar. Continue whisking until medium peaks form, then set aside. In a heavy saucepan set over medium-high heat, bring remaining ½ cup sugar and water to a boil. Do not stir this mixture at any point. Cook until syrup reaches the soft-ball stage or 240° on a candy thermometer. With mixer running, pour boiling syrup in a steady stream into the egg whites. Whip until meringue is cool and forms firm peaks. Stir in vanilla. Spread chilled filling into crust and top with meringue. Top with extra toasted coconut.

— Charlotte Fekete, Birmingham, Alabama

100-year-old Chess Pie

Our State, November 2009

- 3 eggs
- 1½ cups sugar
- 1 stick butter, melted
- 1 Tbsp. vinegar
- 1 tsp. vanilla extract
- ½ cup coconut (optional)
- ½ cup chopped pecans (optional)
- ½ cup raisins (optional)

Beat eggs well. Gradually stir in sugar, butter, and vinegar. Blend until smooth. Add vanilla, coconut, pecans, and raisins. Stir until evenly distributed. Divide filling between two unbaked pastry pie shells. Bake at 350° for 40 minutes.

Phil Cox of Rolesville has been making his specialty pie since getting the recipe from a waitress many years ago.

Harvest Watermelon Pie | Serves 8

Our State, September 1999

- 3 cups chopped watermelon rind (green peel removed)
- 1 package (6 ounces) sweetened dried cranberries
- ¾ cup chopped walnuts
- ½ cup sugar
- ⅓ cup cider vinegar
- 2 tsp. pumpkin pie spice
- 1 tsp. flour
- ¼ tsp. salt
- 1 package (5 ounces) refrigerated pie crusts, room temperature

Orange Glaze
Stir together ½ cup powdered sugar, 2 tsp. grated orange peel, and 1 Tbsp. orange juice.

Place rind in saucepan; add water to cover. Heat to boiling; reduce heat and simmer until translucent and tender, about 10 minutes. Remove from heat and drain. Heat oven to 425°. Stir together cooked rind, cranberries, walnuts, sugar, vinegar, pumpkin pie spice, flour, and salt. Fit one crust into a 9-inch glass pie pan. Pour rind mixture into crust. Cut remaining crust into ½-inch-wide strips; arrange strips over filling to make a lattice crust. Press ends of strips into the edge of the bottom crust over strips. Seal and flute edge. Bake until filling bubbles and crust is browned, about 40 minutes. Cover edge with aluminum foil during baking to prevent excessive browning. Remove pie from oven; spoon orange glaze over hot pie.

— North Carolina Watermelon Association

Old-Fashioned Egg Custard Pie

Our State, April 1993

- 1 cup, plus 1 tsp. sugar
- 3 eggs
- 2 cups milk
- 2 Tbsp. melted butter
- 1 tsp. vanilla
- 1 tsp. flour
- 1 9-inch unbaked pie shell

Set aside 1 teaspoon sugar. Whip remaining 1 cup sugar with eggs until creamy. Beat in milk, melted butter, and vanilla. Combine the reserved sugar with the flour and sprinkle evenly over the pie shell before filling. Heat oven to 300°. Ladle custard into pie shell, and bake until firm, about 40 minutes.

Susan Rogers of Rome, Georgia, sent in her recipe, saying "This recipe is more than 100 years old, and I have used it for more than 15 years with never a failure." A tip: Rogers makes one change to the recipe, which is given here as it was originally written. "I add approximately one teaspoon of ground nutmeg to the filling. This is optional, but I believe it makes a more interesting taste."

Jarrett House Vinegar Pie

Our State, February 1994

- 1 stick margarine, melted and cooled
- 1½ cup sugar
- 1 Tbsp. flour
- 1 Tbsp. vanilla
- 2 Tbsp. apple cider vinegar
- 3 eggs
- 1 9-inch unbaked pie shell

Combine the 6 ingredients and pour into unbaked pie shell. Bake at 300° for 45 minutes.

Diners have been flocking to this inn and restaurant in Dillsboro for more than 100 years. During a visit, it goes without saying that you'll have a bite of their famous Vinegar Pie. If you're not in the area, try making one for yourself, using the Jarrett House's recipe.

Our Favorite Fresh Strawberry Pie | Serves 8

Our State, May 2007

1 cup sugar

5 Tbsp. cornstarch

7 ounces of 7-Up soda

1 quart whole strawberries, cleaned and stems removed

red food coloring, if desired

baked, cooled pie shell

whipped cream, if desired

Blend sugar and cornstarch; add 7-Up. Cook over medium heat, stirring until smooth and thick. Add strawberries and cook for a few minutes. If desired, add red food coloring. Pour into cooled pie shell. Chill. Top with whipped cream, if desired.

— Sweet Tooth: Down-Home Meals & Blue Ribbon Desserts *by Sarah Ann Spaugh, Carolina Avenue Press, Boonville, N.C. 2004.*

Strawberry Pie | Serves 8

Our State, May 1998

¼ cup sugar

2 Tbsp. cornstarch

⅓ cup water

⅓ cup grenadine syrup

1 Tbsp. lemon juice

½ cup sliced, toasted almonds

9-inch baked pie crust

1 package (3.4 ounces) instant vanilla pudding mix

1¼ cups milk

1 cup sour cream

1 pint fresh strawberries, rinsed, sliced

To make glaze for pie, combine sugar and cornstarch in a small saucepan. Stir in water, grenadine, and lemon juice. Cook, stirring constantly, over medium heat until mixture thickens and bubbles. Cover pan and cool to room temperature. Do not refrigerate. Sprinkle almonds evenly over bottom of pie crust. Set aside. In a small bowl, combine pudding mix, milk, and sour cream. Beat at lowest speed of mixer for 1 minute. Immediately pour over almonds in pie crust. Pour ⅓ of glaze over pudding. Arrange strawberries in a circular pattern, beginning next to crust and working toward center of pie. Spoon remaining glaze evenly over top. Refrigerate at least one hour before serving.

— Edie Low, Rock Hill, S.C.

Apple Cobbler | Serves 6-8

Our State, September 2009

Filling

- 6 small red apples, each cored and cut into 8 wedges
- ⅓ cup granulated sugar
- ¼ cup light brown sugar
- ¼ cup orange juice
- ¼ cup all-purpose flour
- 1 tsp. vanilla extract
- 4 Tbsp. cold unsalted butter, diced

Topping

- 1½ cups all-purpose flour
- ⅓ cup granulated sugar
- 2½ tsp. baking powder
- ⅛ tsp. salt
- 5 Tbsp. cold unsalted butter, diced
- 1 cup buttermilk

To finish

- 1 Tbsp. granulated sugar

Preheat oven to 350°. In a large bowl, toss together ingredients for filling — apple wedges, sugar, brown sugar, orange juice, flour, vanilla, and diced butter. Transfer to a 13-x-9-inch baking dish; set aside while preparing topping.

Stir together flour, sugar, baking powder, and salt in a large bowl. Using 2 forks, incorporate diced butter into flour mixture until butter is in small, flaky pieces and mixture resembles coarse cornmeal.

Slowly stir in buttermilk until just combined. Smooth batter evenly over filling, and sprinkle the 1 tablespoon of finishing sugar over the top.

Transfer to oven, and bake for about 1 hour and 15 minutes, or until topping is lightly browned and apples are tender. Let cool slightly, and serve with ice cream.

— Charlotte Fekete, Birmingham, Alabama

Peach Blueberry Cobbler

Our State, July 2006

- ¼ cup sugar
- ¼ cup brown sugar
- 1 Tbsp. cornstarch
- ½ cup water
- 1 Tbsp. lemon juice
- 2 cups sliced peaches
- 1 cup blueberries
- 1 cup all-purpose flour
- ½ cup sugar
- 1½ tsp. baking powder
- ½ tsp. salt
- ¼ cup melted butter

Preheat oven to 375°. Lightly grease an 8-inch square pan. Combine first three ingredients in saucepan. Add water, and cook over medium heat until thick. Remove from heat, and stir in lemon juice, peaches, and blueberries. Pour into prepared pan. In mixer, combine remaining ingredients. Beat until smooth. Spoon batter over fruit. Bake 40 minutes or until crust is brown. Serve warm with a scoop of vanilla ice cream.

— Thyme and Tradition, *Christ School, Arden, N.C., 2001.*

Blueberry Buckle

Our State, October 1999

- ½ cup butter, divided
- 1¼ cups sugar, divided
- 1 egg
- 2⅓ cups all-purpose flour, divided
- 2 tsp. baking powder
- ½ tsp. salt
- ½ cup milk
- 2 cups blueberries
- ½ Tbsp. cinnamon
- Half-and-half or vanilla ice cream

Cream ¼ cup butter with ¾ cup sugar until light and fluffy. Beat egg slightly, then add to mixture, beating well. Sift together the flour, baking powder, and salt. Add 2 cups flour mixture, a little at a time, alternately with milk, beating until smooth after each addition. Fold in blueberries. Spoon batter into a greased 9-x-12-x-2-inch dish. Cream remaining ¼ cup butter with remaining ½ cup sugar, ⅓ cup flour, and cinnamon, blending well. Mixture should be crumbly. Sprinkle evenly over top of blueberry batter. Bake at 375° for 35 minutes. Serve warm with half-and-half or ice cream.

— Marcie Evans, Burgaw

Bob Garner's Peach Cobbler

Our State, May 2008

Filling

3 1-pound bags of frozen, unsweetened peaches (or 7 cups sliced, fresh peaches)

2 cups sugar

⅓ cup butter, melted

4 Tbsp. flour

Grated zest of 1 small lemon

Juice of 1 small lemon

Crust

3 cups flour

1½ tsp. salt

2 sticks (1 cup) softened butter, cut into ½-inch slices

7-8 tsp. ice water

Note: If you prefer a more biscuit-like crust, substitute self-rising flour for the regular flour, add 4 Tbsp. of sugar to the flour, and eliminate the salt. Substitute milk for ice water, but otherwise prepare the pastry the same way as described in recipe.

Sift flour, and mix with salt. Using a pastry cutter, fork, or fingers, cut or work butter into flour until the mixture is in even bits about the size of small peas. Gradually add ice water, and mix lightly with a fork until the mixture begins to form into a ball. Form into a ball, wrap in plastic wrap, and chill in freezer for 5 minutes.

Thaw peaches, if frozen. In a mixing bowl, combine peaches, sugar, flour, melted butter, lemon zest, and lemon juice, and mix thoroughly. Spread ½ of the filling mixture in the bottom of a 9-x-12-inch glass baking dish.

Remove pastry from freezer, and divide into two pieces. Roll or pat out to a normal pie crust thickness and cut into ½-inch strips, laying the strips across the first layer of peaches. Roll out the remaining pastry and cut it into strips. Pour the remaining fruit into the baking dish, and lay the remaining pastry strips atop the fruit. Bake at 425° for 10 minutes, then reduce heat to 350° and bake an additional 50 minutes or until golden brown. Cool; serve topped with vanilla ice cream or whipped cream.

Longtime Our State *contributor Bob Garner is known for his barbecue expertise. Here, he tries his hand at a meal finisher, saying, "This cobbler has a bright, fresh taste due to the lemon zest and lemon juice and doesn't seem overly sweet, which, in my opinion, makes it the perfect accompaniment to a smoky barbecue meal."*

Rustic Peach Tarts | Makes 4 tarts

Our State, August 2008

Crust

2 cups all-purpose flour

¼ tsp. salt

12 Tbsp. (1½ sticks) cold butter, diced

⅓ cup ice-cold water

Filling

1½ pounds peaches, peeled and each cut into 12 wedges

⅓ cup granulated sugar

juice of 1 lemon, about 2 Tbsp.

¼ tsp. vanilla extract

1 egg, beaten with 2 Tbsp. milk

1 Tbsp. granulated sugar

Crust

Toss flour and salt together in a large bowl. Cut diced butter into flour using two knives or a pastry blender. Be sure to disperse the butter throughout the flour; do not blend it in. Once the butter cubes are the size of small peas, slowly add water by the tablespoon until dough forms a shaggy mass. Dough should not be wet and should barely hold together. (Dough can also be made in a stand mixer fitted with the paddle attachment.) Divide dough into 4 equal-sized balls, and wrap each individually in plastic wrap. Refrigerate dough at least 30 minutes.

Filling

Preheat oven to 400°. In a large bowl, toss peaches with sugar, lemon juice, and vanilla; set aside. On a lightly floured surface, roll out each chilled dough ball into an 8-inch round, about 1/4-inch thick. Transfer rounds to 2 parchment-lined baking sheets, and mound equal portions of filling into the center of each tart. Fold the edges of the dough in toward the center (dough will cover part of filling), pinching and folding to create a pleated edge. Brush crust with egg mixture, and sprinkle sugar over crust. Bake for 30-40 minutes or until peaches are tender and crust is browned.

— Charlotte Fekete, Birmingham, Alabama

Lemony Peach and Blueberry Crisp | Serves 4-6

Our State, August 2008

Filling

3 pounds peaches, each cut into 8 wedges, peeled (optional)

1 cup blueberries

grated zest and juice of 2 lemons

¼ cup granulated sugar

2 Tbsp. all-purpose flour

Topping

¾ cup all-purpose flour

¾ cup old-fashioned oats

¼ cup light brown sugar

¼ cup granulated sugar

¼ tsp. salt

8 Tbsp. (1 stick) cold butter, diced

Preheat oven to 350°. In a large bowl, toss peaches, blueberries, lemon zest and juice, sugar, and flour together; transfer to a medium-size baking dish.

To make the topping, combine flour, oats, both sugars, and salt in a large bowl and stir to combine. Add diced butter, and work into the flour mixture using two knives or a pastry blender until butter is the size of small peas and mixture is crumbly. Sprinkle topping over peach mixture, and bake for 45-55 minutes or until crispy and bubbly.

— Charlotte Fekete, Birmingham, Alabama

Insanely Easy Blackberry Cobbler | Makes 10 servings

Our State, August 2003

½ cup butter

2 cups self-rising flour

2 cups white sugar

2 cups milk

3½ cups blackberries

Preheat oven to 350°. Place butter in 9-x-13-inch baking pan; melt in oven. In a medium bowl, stir together the flour, sugar, and milk until lumpy. Pour mixture on top of melted butter in baking pan. Do not stir butter and mixture together. Drop blackberries into batter. Bake for 1 hour or until golden brown.

— Wendy Faulkner

No-Bake Blueberry Sonker

Our State, September 2005

4 pints fresh blueberries

1¼ cups sugar

4 large cooked biscuits

Dip:

¾ cup sugar

¼ cup cornstarch

4 cups (1 quart) whole milk

¾ tsp. vanilla

Combine blueberries and 1¼ cups sugar in large bowl, mashing slightly to release juices. Tear biscuits into hunks about thumb-sized, and stir into berry mixture. Cover and refrigerate 8 hours or overnight. When ready to serve, bring sonker to room temperature as you prepare the dip. Whisk together ¾ cup sugar and cornstarch, then stir into milk, leaving no lumps. Stir in vanilla. In a double boiler over simmering water, or in a heavy-bottomed pan over medium-low heat, cook, stirring constantly, until the mixture is smooth and thickened. Do not boil. Let the dip cool slightly, and pass around the table for diners to pour over individual servings of sonker.

The sonker — a deep-dish pie traditionally baked in a biscuit tin — has a yearly festival devoted to it in Lowgap, near Mount Airy, held on the first Saturday in October at the Edwards-Franklin House.

Maxine Dockery's Sweet Potato Sonker

Our State, September 2005

6 to 8 sweet potatoes, cooked and peeled

3 to 4 cups sugar

3 to 4 cups self-rising flour

½ pound (1 cup) butter

pastry to cover top of pan

Use a baking pan that's 11-x-13 inches and three or more inches deep. Cover the bottom of the pan with a layer of sliced sweet potatoes. Sprinkle with sugar and flour, and dot with butter. Continue making layers until the pan is filled. Top with a layer of pastry. Bake in a 400° oven for 40 minutes or until the pastry is done.

Topping: Stir ½ cup or more of granulated sugar into 1 to 2 cups sweet milk; heat, stirring. Remove from heat, and add 1 tsp. vanilla. Pour the hot topping over the hot sonker. Serve warm.

— North Carolina and Old Salem Cookery *by Beth Tartan, UNC Press, 1992.*

Individual Pecan-and-Chocolate Tarts

Our State, December 2008

1 recipe basic tart dough, chilled (see below)

¾ cup light brown sugar

¼ cup light corn syrup

1½ Tbsp. unsalted butter, melted

2 large eggs

1 tsp. vanilla extract

⅛ tsp. salt

1½ cups pecan halves

¾ cup semisweet chocolate chips

Basic Tart Dough:

8 Tbsp. unsalted butter, softened

½ cup granulated sugar

2 large egg yolks

1 tsp. water

¼ tsp. salt

1⅓ cups all-purpose flour

Preheat oven to 350°. On a lightly floured board, gently knead and divide tart dough into 4- equal-sized balls. Roll out each ball into a 6-inch round, about ⅛ -inch-thick, and press into 4 lightly greased 4¼-inch fluted tart pans with removable bottoms. Trim edges, and prick bases all over with fork. Let shells chill in refrigerator for 15 minutes, and then bake until set and lightly browned, about 15 minutes. Let cool while preparing filling.

In a large bowl, whisk together brown sugar, corn syrup, and melted butter. Whisk in eggs, vanilla, and salt; stir in pecans and chocolate chips. Divide filling between tart shells. Bake for 30 to 35 minutes or until crust is golden brown and filling is bubbly. Let cool slightly before serving.

Basic Tart Dough

In the bowl of an electric mixer fitted with the paddle attachment, beat butter and sugar together until creamy. Add egg yolks, water, and salt; mix to combine. Add flour, and mix until dough is moist and in several medium-sized clumps. Using your hands, form dough into a ball and flatten slightly into a disc. Wrap dough tightly with plastic wrap, and chill until completely firm, about 2 hours. Makes 1 disc, enough for one 9-inch tart or four 4¼-inch tarts.

— Charlotte Fekete, Birmingham, Alabama

Blueberry Tart | Serves 8

Our State, August 1997

Crust

1 stick unsalted butter (4 ounces), melted and cooled

½ cup sugar

⅛ tsp. pure lemon extract

⅛ tsp. pure vanilla extract

a pinch of salt

1¼ cups of unbleached all-purpose flour

Filling

½ cup heavy cream

1 large egg

¼ cup mascarpone cheese

½ tsp. pure lemon extract

½ tsp. pure vanilla extract

2 Tbsp. flavorful honey (blueberry, sourwood, or tulip poplar)

3 tsp. flour

Topping

1 pint fresh blueberries or other berries

confectioners sugar for dusting

Preheat oven to 375°. Butter a 9-inch tart pan with removable bottom. Mix melted butter and sugar together with a wooden spoon. Add extracts, salt, and 1¼ cups flour. Continue to stir until mixture is the consistency of cookie dough. Turn dough out into buttered tart pan. Press dough evenly onto the bottom and side of pan. The dough should be thin and evenly distributed. Cover dough with foil wrap and either dried beans or pie weights.

Bake in hot oven for 12 to 15 minutes until crust begins to turn brown. Remove foil and weights, continue to bake for another 3-5 minutes until crust is browned.

Meanwhile, prepare filling by whisking together cream, egg, cheese, extracts, and honey until smooth. Add remaining flour, one tsp. at a time, whisking between teaspoons until smooth and well blended. Pour filling into pre-baked crust.

Bake in hot oven until filling is firm and the pastry is a deep golden brown. Remove from oven and allow to cool. Arrange berries in a single layer over filling.

Dust with confectioners sugar and serve with blueberry honey ice cream (recipe on page 71).

In 1997, Nancy Quaintance of Greensboro wrote Our State*'s "Tar Heel Living" column.*